ART
TALK

ART TALK

A Practical Guide to
Painting and Drawing

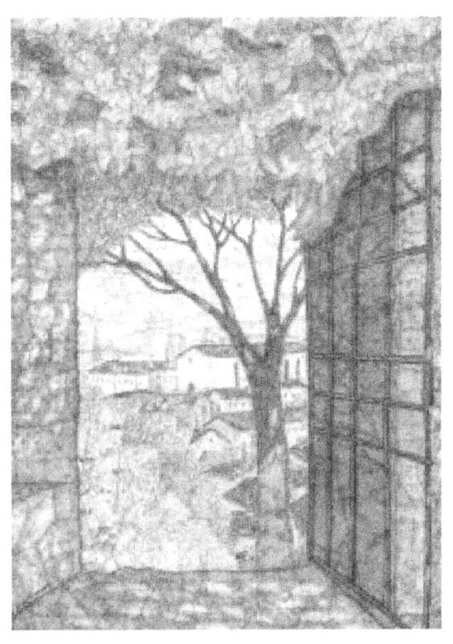

Eileen Potter Kopelman

ISBN 0-7414-2533-5

Cover design by Zaminy@splendidlyhip.com
Photo of the author □ by Jonas; used with permission
All drawings □ by E.P. Kopelman

Published by:

INFI∞ITY
PUBLISHING.COM

1094 New De Haven Street, Suite 100
West Conshohocken, PA 19428-2713
Info@buybooksontheweb.com
www.buybooksontheweb.com
Toll-free (877) BUY BOOK
Local Phone (610) 941-9999
Fax (610) 941-9959

Printed in the United States of America

Printed on Recycled Paper

Published June 2005

Special thanks to my parents, siblings, and husband for being great patrons of my art, to my niece Zaminy@splendidlyhip.com for her help with the cover, to my friends, Jane, a teacher; Anna, an artist; Christine, a poet; and Gaynell, an artist; for critiquing the manuscript, and to Carol, an artist and teacher, for being there when I was ready to learn about art.

Eileen Kopelman
New Kensington, Pennsylvania
March 1, 2005

Contents

✸ *Getting Started* 1

    Adding Art to Our Lives 3

    Workshops and Private Lessons 9

    The Studio.................................... 11

    The Painting in your Mind's Eye 18

    Story Telling and Drama 19

    Thumbnail Sketches 22

✸ *Painting and Drawing*.................................... 25

    Watercolor 27

    Color.................................... 32

    Oils and Acrylics.................................... 36

    Watercolor Paper 39

    Pen and Ink.................................... 42

    Pastels.................................... 46

    Colored Pencils 48

    Conte Crayons.................................... 49

    Charcoal.................................... 50

✸ *Problem Solving*.................................... 51

    The Painting Process 53

    Transposing Images to Painting Surfaces 54

    Measuring and Positioning 57

    Negative Space.................................... 58

    Composition.................................... 59

    Perspective.................................... 61

    People in Paintings.................................... 62

The Checkerboard 65

Interior Perspective 67

Drawing Round Vases and Tables...................69

Roof Peaks 71

Basic House 73

Row Houses 75

Roofs on Row Houses...77

Barn Roofs 79

Pennsylvania Bank Barn....................................82

Buildings on a Hillside 84

Perspective from Above 86

✳ *How to Paint Things* 89

Portraits...91

Painting Things that are White.......................98

Fog 99

Shadows...100

Clouds 101

Smoke...102

Snow 103

Outdoor (Plein Air) Painting 105

Water 109

Reflections 112

Windows...115

Left Sides...116

Trees 117

Flowers...121

Birds..123

Rocks 125

Beaches...127

Atmospheric Perspective...130
Painting When You Travel...131

✸ *Odds and Ends*... 135

Matting and Framing.....................................137
Giclee Prints 141
Hand Made Paper 143
Painted Sculptures...146
Building a Web Site 147
Art Clubs, Guilds and Galleries 150
Bon Voyage...153
Magazines...154
Vendors...155

✸ *Bibliography*... 156

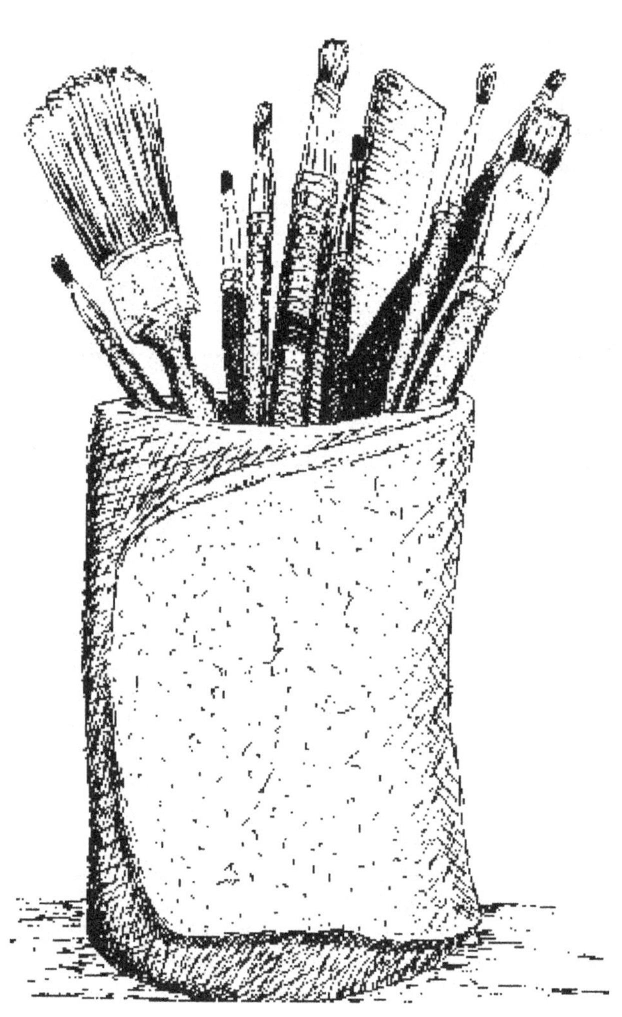

Getting Started

- **Adding Art to Our Lives**
- **Workshops and Private Lessons**
- **The Studio**
- **The Painting in your Mind's Eye**
- **Story Telling and Drama**
- **Thumbnail Sketches**

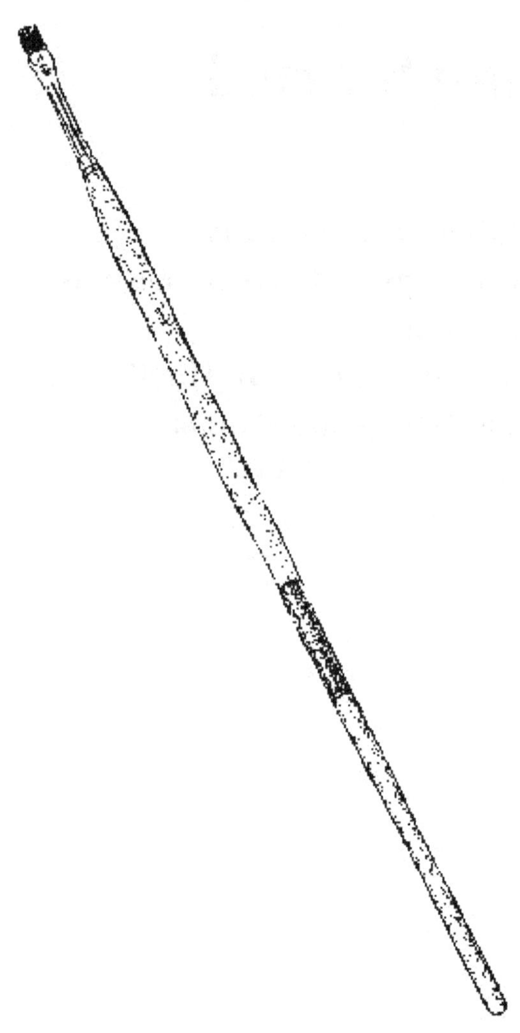

No. 1 Bright for Oil Painting

Adding Art to Our Lives

If you have always liked art, and would like to learn to paint but have never had much instruction, then I have written this book for you. Your artistic trip through life can be an enjoyable one. The Greek poet Constantino Kavafis (1863-1933) (Anglicized as Constantine Cavafy) wrote of the journey to Ithaka. [Ref. 13, p.67] He tells us to enjoy the ports along the way and to have a marvelous time getting there. Ithaka can be interpreted as any ultimate goal of life, even death, or in the artist's life, a masterpiece. Pursuing this goal can lead to a very happy life, provided the artist does not despair each day that the masterpiece does not materialize. As a painter you will see things that others do not, and the things others see, you will see differently. Painting is a pleasant pastime. It can be your occupation or your hobby. Paint at any age, from youth into the golden years. If you like it, stick to it, and are reasonably satisfied with your efforts, your life's journey will be richer for the experience.

Artists often make a living by teaching as well as painting. Some give lessons from their homes while others teach in more structured high school or college settings. Some find very creative ways to fulfill their own painting ambitions as well as teach. One artist with whom I am acquainted teaches college art classes during the school year and applies for grants which pay his way to exotic far off places where he paints during the summer. His art provides a steady income, helps the younger generation learn about art, and gives him an interesting life.

This book is a teaching tool. As a student and an artist I have both experienced problems and observed others having difficulties in certain areas of painting and drawing. "Art Talk" includes thumbnail sketches, transposing photos to a painting surface, watercolors and other media, how to position roof peaks, barn roofs, buildings on a hillside, how to paint reflections, fog, snow, shadows, how to set up a studio, paint when you travel, and more. This book addresses many problems in art and will show you how to solve them.

I learned to paint after a twenty year career as a retail clothing buyer. When one leaves a regular job, forty plus or minus hours a week suddenly become free time. One has to make new choices and develop a new routine. The choices seem to narrow down to playing golf, bridge, or getting into other hobbies and clubs. Retirement can be a fun time for doing things that were impossible to do while working. I read somewhere that one in four retirees takes up painting. When making a living is no longer a primary focus, artwork can be an outlet for productive excess energy. I often take my art supplies on vacation. Art, especially drawing and watercolor, is portable. There is no age limit and there is the chance that you can be famous, or at least remembered, when you are dead because your work will live on.

A friend of mine, who paints in oils, says, "art is about color, design, unity, personal expression, clarity, beauty, light and shadow." All those things need to come together with some practical knowledge to make them work as a unit. An artist needs to understand how to use painting and drawing materials. Without encouragement and a few tips one might attempt to paint a picture, end up with bad results, become discouraged, and let the paints, crayons, or pencils, rest untouched in a drawer for years. It has happened to me in the past and perhaps to you as well.

Other, narrowly focused, instructional books about painting often contain pretty pictures with only a few lines of real information about how to paint. The goal of this book is to put knowledge about painting in your head before you touch pencil to paper or brush to canvas. As you read, you will learn the painting techniques I have learned. You will reach an understanding of how to use various products and how to paint subjects that once seemed difficult. You will understand the process of creating pictures in your mind's eye and painting them. You will find out how to set up your studio and what products might be useful to you. When you have finished reading, you will have an overview of various painting media and the confidence to try those that interest you.

Why do people always ask "How long did it take you to paint that?" It happens just about every time I show my work. If you haven't heard this question, you surely will. They ask the question as if the time involved were the key to a successful painting, and as if you should know the answer. They seem to think that the artist keeps a log or works on one painting exclusively until it is finished. Maybe they think the painting in the artist's mind just morphs out onto the canvas or paper with no effort and with as much speed as possible. Perhaps, they imagine, if they spent the same amount of time on their own painting, they could do the same thing. Maybe they could, but not without some study and practice. Notwithstanding the shortcuts made possible with computers, it just doesn't happen that way. One thing is certain, it takes less time if you work at it more. I mean, of course, that if you don't work on your painting, it will take you forever to finish it. Paintings take planning and some work. If you want to paint, you can and will do it, but you have to get started and then spend time doing it. Producing a painting can take any amount of time.

What is great art? Will you know a great painting when you see it? Or when you paint it? Maybe; maybe not. It may take a few days before you realize you can't forget a painting you have seen and then you'll know it was a good one. Pennsylvania's Governor Rendell signed legislation at his desk as a newspaper photographer took the picture in color. A large, wonderful painting of an American flag was hanging on the wall behind the Governor and the desk caught its reflection. I knew it was better than the old flag paintings I had seen by another, better known artist. I found out later that the painting was done by a Philadelphia pop artist named John Stango. (http://www.stango.com) The flag was stunning. It had flecks of bright green and orange through it. Some of the stars were those colors, too. It was fabulous. Great paintings are not done overnight. It takes most artists a long time to become well known. That said, however, you don't need to think your work is bad just because you are new at it. You may look at your early work years from now and smile and think, "Not bad!"

A critic once wrote that Pablo Picasso (1881-1973) should have thrown away part of his work and the world would have been better off. Some artists find it therapeutic to get rid of lesser works. If you decide to get rid of work that you think is sub-standard, do it in stages. Move those paintings and drawings to a "re-cycle bin" for a couple of years. Look at them again and see if you agree with your original decision. If you are going to throw things away, let some time pass and take a fresh look at the work before you get rid of it, otherwise you may regret the decision. I threw away one of my paintings because a workshop teacher was not very encouraging. Later I decided I liked my work better than the teacher's. I still miss the painting. Pop artist, Andy Warhol, kept everything from ticket stubs to work he did for hire, and they built a museum for him. Of course, it helped that he interviewed celebrities in his own magazine and attained great fame from doing so. My best thought on this is never throw any of your work away.

Until middle age my art education was minimal. I took an art appreciation class in college. I bought watercolor paints but quit after one try because I didn't know how to properly use them. Prior to that I had only one moment of artistic enlightenment. It occurred during one of only two art classes I had in high school when I realized artists had their own individual styles of painting. The assignment was to identify artists by their painting styles. A friend and I rushed to the school library during a rare study hall. It was the first and last time we were ever in there due to our heavy extra-curricular schedules. We found books about Monet, Mondrian, Cezanne, van Gogh, and others and it dawned on us that this was a doable assignment. We aced the test.

The best way to learn about art is to look at great paintings and read books about the artists who painted them. Books, magazines, libraries and museums all have the information. Museums rarely show watercolors because the old pigments often fade when exposed to light. New paints may hold up better. They do exhibit oil paintings. Look closely. Some of them are magnificent. Streaks and bits of odd shades mix with the predominant colors in the paintings. Let the paintings of the masters lead your eyes through a delightful mix of colorful surprises. Magazines and books have pictures of the same paintings, but the colors are truer and more interesting in the original works. Even prints available for sale in museum shops do not capture all the nuances visible in the original paintings.

If you need structure or companionship in your painting life, take some lessons or a workshop. Be careful not to copy the teacher's style. Sometimes you may not feel like painting. Without lessons or workshops, it might be easy to take a break from painting that could last for years. There will always be something more pressing that requires your attention. With some type of artistic routine built into your schedule, you will find that even with a bout of artist's block that causes you not to paint when you're home by yourself, you will paint at the lesson every week. It will keep you involved with painting even if you don't feel much like it, and when you are energized once again, it will be right there for you. Join an art club and learn from the artists around you. Often small ancillary groups paint together somewhere once a week. Sometimes it takes me forever to sit down at my painting table, but once I get there, I can paint for two or three hours and have no idea that so much time has elapsed. Painting is therapeutic. It clears the mind and makes one pay rapt attention to the work for quite a while. If you build painting time into your schedule, you may find it easier to get started and maintain your interest in art. Art will then become your focus and will not be left out of the daily routine and lost.

Workshops and Private Lessons

Workshops and lessons can make up for a lack of formal schooling in art. You may have had to dig out the information you needed long after graduation as I did. This is not always a bad thing. If your school focused on a fad like installation art or taught abstract art without teaching basic drawing and painting skills, then education in that school would have been pretty much a waste of time. In case you are unfamiliar with installation art, it can be summed up by saying that if you were to see a plaster of Paris leg hanging over a table in the corner of a room, you would be looking at installation art. It is a way to fill up a room or exhibit space without much effort. It requires large items and one or two artists. Foundations and public monies pay for it. In most cases nobody buys it, and when the show is over, it is discarded. It is useless. I guess you can tell that I don't care much for installation art. That's a workshop I would skip.

As I learned in high school every painter, who does not simply copy someone else's work, gradually develops an identifiable style. As you progress you will develop one. Learn from, but don't slavishly copy, the painting styles of others. Take bits and pieces of those you like and incorporate them into your own paintings. Every painter who is starting out needs guidance from someone who knows how to help produce the desired results. Take lessons, visit museums, read fine art magazines and books. Go to art shows. See what others have done and are doing.

My art teacher teaches art like piano teachers teach piano. One student at a time. Whether it's a half-hour or a two hour lesson, it is individualized instruction. I have taken an occasional workshop or class in the past, primarily to see what else is available, and also for the companionship of other artists. I have observed that most workshop teachers have a difficult time finding something an entire class can do because people who attend workshops often have different skill levels. Even so, if I learn one new thing at a workshop, I feel it has not been a waste of time. I progress much faster in a private lesson, however, than I do in a workshop. The workshops are usually cheaper per hour, but they waste a lot of time. If you are lucky enough to find a teacher who can answer all your painting questions and who will help you achieve the results you want, keep taking lessons from that teacher. Continuity is important and the teacher can help you go where your interests lead. Workshops aren't geared to do that. However you do it, the main thing is to learn to draw and paint and have fun while you are doing it. Art schools encourage students to find something that makes their work unique, distinguishes it from the work of others, and makes it get noticed. While this is necessary to a point, high quality work will make you better known over time than cheap, shock effect methods that produce the fifteen minutes of fame that Andy Warhol said everybody will get in their lifetime. Don't think you have failed if your painting does not look like your instructor's. The goal is not to be a clone. If others begin to identify your work as your teacher's, you might want to think about finding a new one.

The Studio

My art room/studio started out in a small way as a spare room where I sketched and painted. After a couple of years it became obvious that the spare room furniture would have to go to the basement, and I had an art room. It only worked because we don't get a lot of company. Other artists' studios, including those of friends, have always intrigued me. The only famous artist's studio I have visited is Winslow Homer's (1836-1910), which is open to the public, in Prout's Neck, Maine. I saw it ninety years after his death. By then it was a large, rather musty room with high ceilings, but in its day, it must have been grand. Mine is a small garden variety spare room that will never have enough room for all my art supplies. Any room you choose for your studio will probably not be big enough, not have enough storage space, or have other problems. Our belongings expand to fill the space we allow for them. Comedian, George Carlin, did a whole routine on one's "stuff." It still rings true. The trappings of an art career or hobby can sneak up on you. My friends and I joke that our real career is buying art supplies. If we live to be a hundred, we cannot possibly use all the products we have bought. We buy new things to try, or so we won't run out of whatever it is, or because it looks like something we would like to use, or maybe it's just an impulse purchase. My studio is well organized. I can find just about everything, and the room works pretty well. Periodically, however, I find that things pile up and I have to sort and pitch. The piling up usually happens when I have a project of some sort that is not art related at all. The offending paperwork seems to arrange itself in stacks on my painting table. When I can't get to the table to paint, the clutter takes time away from my art. Once the project is done, I throw out what I can, start painting again, and check to see if I need any more supplies!

When approaching art as a hobby, think twice before you rush to buy expensive supplies and equipment. You might be better off to wait until you feel a real need for them. Artists' grade paints, permanent inks and archival paper are appropriate if you want your work to last, but wait to buy an expensive easel, or a steel flat file, until you really need it. Informal studies have shown that the more one spends on expensive equipment, the less one enjoys the hobby. [Ref. 8, p. 36] If you really do a lot of painting, let your needs guide you in outfitting your studio.

If you are just getting started, there are a few essentials. A table, chair, paints in a few basic colors, three or four brushes in various sizes, and paper or canvas should be all you need at first. As time goes on your list might include a drafting table, bookshelves, a steel flat file for watercolors and drawings, a magnifier lamp, a light box, an easel if you paint in oil, a small sturdy table and a mat cutter if you plan to make mats for works on paper. You will probably need a large tote bag as well as a case for carrying unfinished watercolors to lessons or to paint elsewhere. A fishing tackle box works well for carrying oil paints. You might find a computer useful for cataloguing and keeping track of your art.

My first piece of art room furniture was an adjustable height drafting table. It can be tilted, raised, or lowered. I already had a small oak table, and later, I found a fold-up masonite and aluminum table. I bought a portable, inexpensive mat cutter and learned how to use it by reading the directions. Soon after that I added a studio easel for oil painting. I have an adjustable chair on wheels to use at my computer as well as at the drafting table. A higher chair or stool might have been a better choice at the drafting table. Two bookshelves and a couple of file cabinets, TV set and an exercise machine complete my fairly crowded room. My most crushing need, which gradually became evident, was to

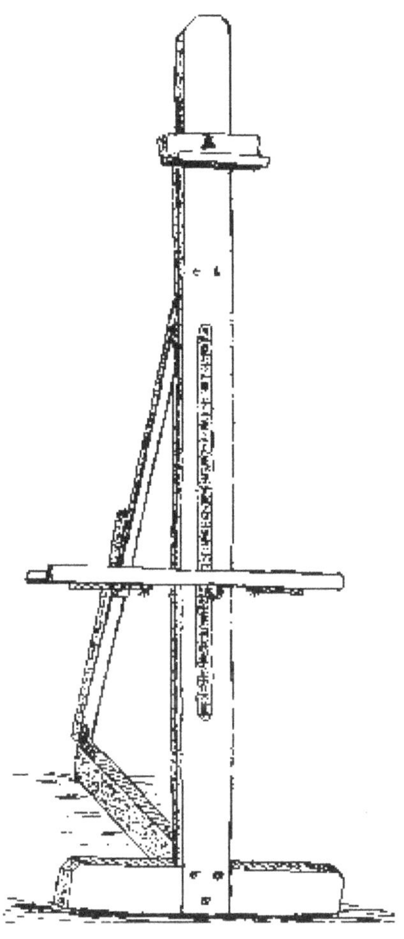

Studio Easel for Oil Painting

find space for finished watercolors, extra books, and miscellaneous supplies. The solution was to empty the closet, put up metal strips and wooden shelving, and buy a steel flat file. The flat file was expensive, but it has been well worth the price. Its five drawers, base area, and space on top are the equivalent of several extra tables for works on paper

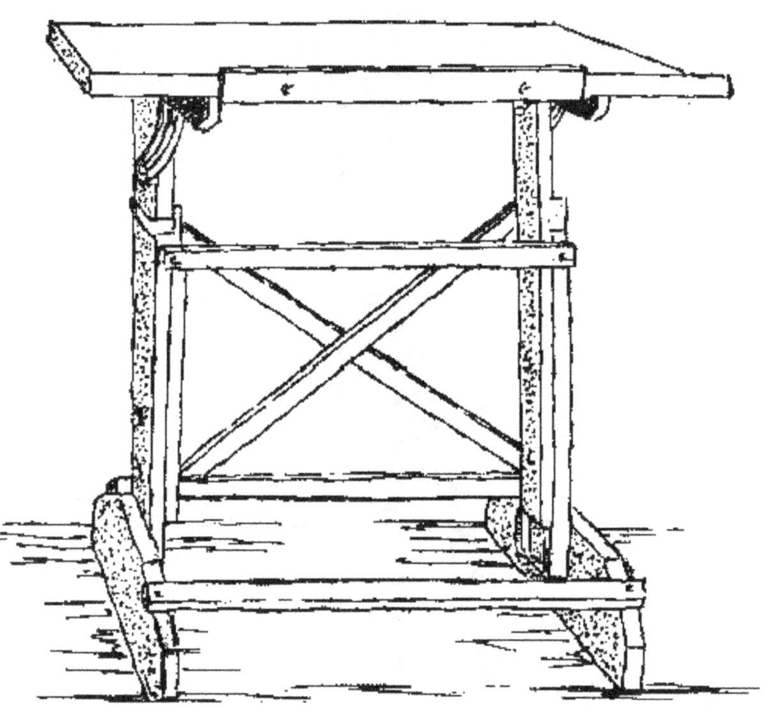

Adjustable Table for Drawing and Painting

that need to be stored unframed and flat. Later I bought a light box and a fluorescent lamp with a magnifier in the center. The lamp clamps onto the drafting table and is very helpful for looking at or painting fine detail. The light box comes in handy when I want to draw the opposite side of a symmetrical object such as a jug or vase.

I take many pictures of things I hope to paint later. They really accumulate. A digital camera is probably the best kind to take on trips because you edit out or print only the best pictures. The danger is that editing might remove a good photo that later you realize you should have kept. Photo storage boxes have helped me eliminate much of the clutter. Label photos on the back in pencil as soon as you print out or develop them. Ink will sometimes leach through and ruin a photo. Other inks may not be permanent and, in time, can fade away completely. Labeling the container box or album is important because it makes finding pictures from specific trips easier. As soon as possible after a trip, I pull out the photos I want to keep for future paintings and keep them in a separate stack. Eventually they end up in their own storage box.

As I painted and framed more work, another problem presented itself. How could I display framed paintings in my studio without damaging the walls? The solution was to install 2 ½ inch crown molding, upside down, about six inches from the ceiling around the room on all four walls. I used brass "S" hooks and poly-cotton brick-layer's cord to hang pictures. One could, I suppose, simply drive nails into the top of the right side up molding and run the cord around them instead of using brass hooks. The cord is available at hardware stores. Make sure it's poly/cotton because the polyester gives added strength. Hang the hooks over the top of the upside down crown molding. This system eliminates the need to constantly drive nails into the walls as you hang new pictures. If you do this in your studio, make sure the molding is upside down so there is a "lip" for the hooks to hang onto, otherwise it won't work the way it should. There are other, more expensive ways to hang work in the studio, but this one works well for me.

Fishing line may look good but it doesn't work well for hanging things. I learned this first from my hanging plants. I'm not sure whether it was the weight of the plants or the heat of the sun or both, but multiple strands of fishing line would hold for a while and then they would break and I

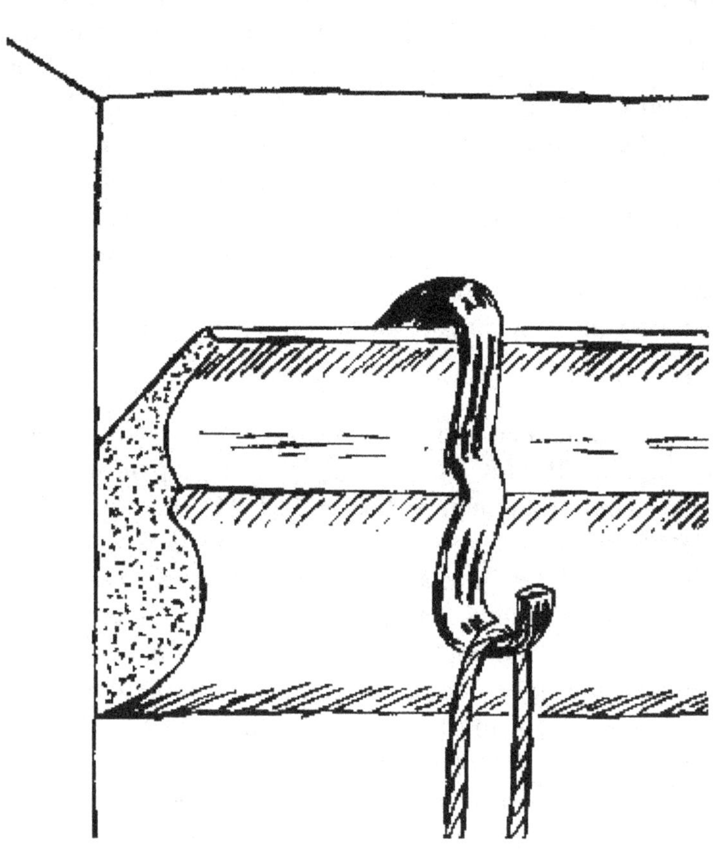

Upside down Crown Molding and Brass Picture Hook

would find a smashed basket and dirt, flowers, and plastic shards on the floor. Later at an East Suburban Artists' League show at a Pittsburgh church, two paintings hung with fishing line came crashing down between the time they went up and the day the show opened. The glass had to be replaced on one of them. Fishing line looks good, but should only be used for a short time with well tied square knots and sufficient tensile strength to hold up the painting if you use it at all.

Prices for studio accessories often vary greatly from place to place. It pays to shop discount, office supply, and art stores as well as their catalogues. Art catalogues may be over priced on things not directly related to art such as office lighting and camping supplies for outdoor painting, but they will often have items, not found locally, that can make your studio more comfortable and efficient. When I shop the catalogues, I tend to be a more thoughtful shopper and buy less on impulse. By the time I pick up the phone or go on-line, I usually have a pretty good idea of what I really need.

Every studio will benefit from having a sink and running water nearby. Even though you may move really messy projects to the kitchen or even outdoors, it is very convenient to have water handy for washing out brushes and filling containers.

Recessed ceiling lighting was the last thing we added to my art room. It was truly a godsend. One recessed ceiling light in each corner area of the room made the whole room light up. If you add this type of lighting to an existing home, i.e. not new construction, be sure to buy fixtures designed for old construction in order to avoid a fire hazard. They are available at home building supply stores. Have a licensed electrician install one or two lights per switch. Good lighting will make a huge difference in how you enjoy and spend time in your studio.

The Painting in your Mind's Eye

The mind's eye needs to have its vision. Great paintings do not just happen because the artist gets up in the morning, clueless, with no idea how the painting will look when it's done, slaps paint on paper or canvas and produces a masterpiece by noon. Imagining how a finished painting will look before it is painted will give you an attainable goal.

There is a wonderful poem that I heard read somewhere years ago about paintings in a great European museum that were removed from their frames for safe-keeping during wartime. It told how the docents described the paintings that had been hanging in each frame, but were no longer there, to the museum's wartime visitors. A curious thing happened. Blind people from the neighborhood started coming to the museum. The docents described every brush stroke and scene from the paintings they knew so well to everyone who came to "see" them. Blind people continued to visit the museum until the war was over and the paintings were re-hung. With the paintings back in their frames, the docents no longer described them in such magnificent detail and the blind people stopped coming.

The mind's eye is a powerful tool that will keep you on track while you paint. Envision your painting clearly before you begin to paint. Of course, it may not turn out exactly as you imagined, but proper planning does produce results. Some artists do very elaborate preliminary work so they know exactly how each painting will turn out.

Story Telling and Drama

My favorite paintings are those that tell a story, either with the action in the painting, or through the title. When I look at those paintings, I don't have to guess or be told by a docent or a catalogue what the artist was trying to convey. A tortured artist may show his misery by painting dismal blobs, but that doesn't make me feel the pain. Nor are my favorites photo-realistic. We have cameras for that. Art made in a painterly fashion is fun to look at and many paintings by well known artists provide good examples of story telling in art.

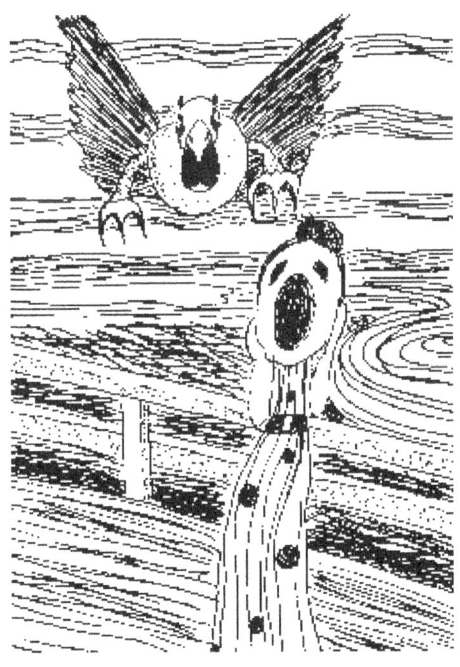

Something to Scream About

Norwegian painter, Edvard Munch's (1863-1944) famous "Scream" paintings usually have a couple of mysterious figures on the walkway some distance behind the screaming person. His paintings make us feel uneasy without knowing the exact reason for our fear. Our imagination fills in the details. Munch's paintings make us wonder what's going on. My version with the big bad bird puts a new twist on it.

Contemporary historical painters John Buxton, (1939-) (buxtonart.com) and Robert Griffing, (1940-) (paramountpress.com) have become successful by accurately portraying life in colonial America, including famous people, Indians, soldiers, battles, clothing, and rifles. [Ref. 17, pp. 2-5, 23] Buxton, who paints with relatively quick drying alkyds, was influenced by his work for National Geographic® where it was crucial to get all the details down correctly. One of Griffing's paintings, based on fact, shows Indians and colonists preparing to dine inside the hollow, thirty foot diameter, trunk of a cottonwood tree with large bark canoes on the riverbank in the foreground. Both artists have done tremendous amounts of research for their work.

Vincent Van Gogh (1853-1890) painted his own time. One of his haying scenes shows two exhausted workers, a young man and a young woman, taking a nap in the shade of a haystack. [Ref. 5, cover] Both are dressed in blue with paint applied in his familiar brush strokes. The girl has a white head covering and the man wears a small straw hat. His simple shoes are in the foreground. The sky is vibrant blue. The haystacks are golden, with darker gold and some blues in the shadows. The girl is asleep on her side, facing the viewer and the young man is on his back. His hands are clasped behind his head and his hat is over his eyes. The energetic, colorful brush strokes mold the shapes and shadows.

Gustave Caillebotte's (1848-1894) painting of workmen sanding a wooden floor with hand sanders shows their sweaty backs glistening as they work in unison. The floorboards shine and the men almost come alive. Look at any construction site. You've probably seen the viewing holes in the fences, put there just so passersby can watch. We like paintings that show people working.

In Charles M. Russell's (1864-1926) "Unexpected Guest," [Ref. 14, p. 107] an idyllic cowboy breakfast is interrupted by a bear up on its hind legs coming towards the campfire from the right side of the painting. One cowboy is asleep. His partner is making a fast grab for his rifle. The horses in the upper left of the picture are trying to get away, and the frying pan and food are flying. There is no need to ask what the artist's message is here.

The Dutch artist Jan Vermeer (1632-1675) conveyed a sense of mystery and concern in some of his paintings of women who are pregnant. One shows a woman reading a letter. Critics often choose to ignore the fact that Vermeer's women sometimes appear to be expectant mothers, but appreciating that fact enhances the drama in the paintings. [Ref. 18, pp. 72, 73]

A title that makes one realize something is amiss such as "Lost on the Outer Banks" by Winslow Homer (1836-1910) can be very effective. A fisherman in a boat surrounded by a foggy ocean suddenly becomes a very frightening situation as you understand that the man has no idea which way to go to find land. The title works. That painting inspired a car commercial in which a lost fisherman presses his remote button and his car lights come on, where it is parked on shore, and he is saved. Homer's fisherman had no such device and his painting transports us to a very scary place.

Thumbnail Sketches

The first thing to make, when you have decided what you want to paint, is a quick thumbnail sketch. A thumbnail sketch is a tiny sketch, your choice, but roughly 1½ inches by 2 or 3 inches, of your painting idea, on a piece of paper proportionately the same size as the paper or canvas painting surface. Transfer the thumbnail sketch as described in the section on transposing images to painting surfaces.

Thumbnail sketches can be quite simple. When I first began to take art lessons, I thought that surely I would never be able to fill up a 22" by 30" whole sheet of watercolor paper with any sort of painting at all. I spent my time painting individual objects. But after drawing and painting "portraits" of things, I found that, as ideas came to me for real paintings, I already knew how to paint the individual items that were going to be part of the new, more involved paintings. If you have never painted before, try painting single items before you paint complicated arrangements. Get in the habit of doing a thumbnail when it's easy to do. Once you do the sketch routinely, complicated paintings will seem more manageable. If the overall design does not work well as a thumbnail sketch it will not, most likely, be an effective painting either. But if it works, your chance of having a well designed painting goes way up.

Sometimes shading objects to give them volume will make the sketch better. You may then see at a glance where you need to strengthen or weaken the dark and light areas to make all parts of the sketch work harmoniously. The reason for doing a thumbnail sketch is to ensure that large elements of the painting work well together while eliminating excess clutter without wasting a lot of time, paint, effort, and paper or canvas. Don't put in much detail. Do it quickly. If you don't like the way your sketch looks, it is very easy to do a dozen others until you find the one that works. Then, when you start the full size drawing, you won't be wasting time rearranging major elements because you will have already solved design problems.

For a color preview, make a fast, rough, imprecise, mock up using colored markers on Bristol board. Bristol board is a heavy, smooth paper that comes in tablets. It shouldn't take very long and will eliminate the need to solve color questions as you paint. This, added to the thumbnail sketch will get your painting off to a good start. As someone once said "A good drawing will never be a bad painting and a bad drawing will never be a good painting."

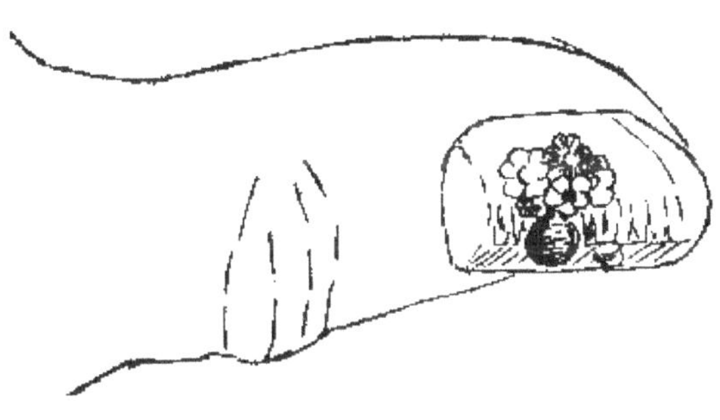

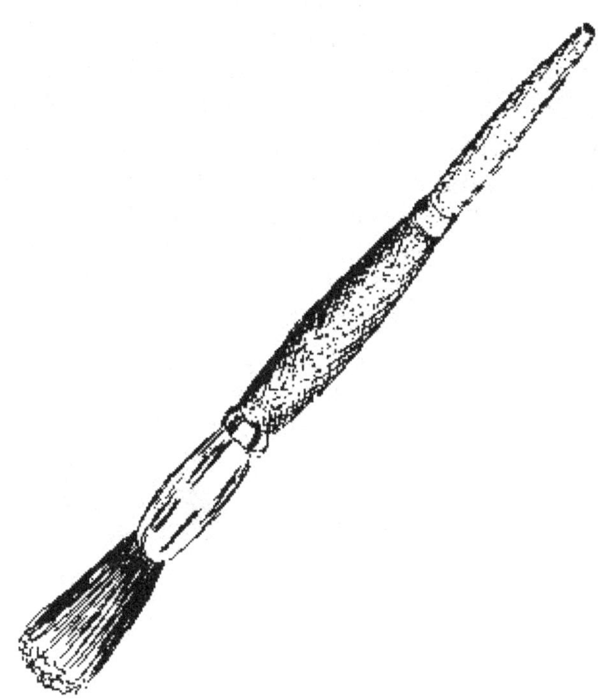

Round Brush for Watercolor Painting

Painting and Drawing

- **Watercolor**
- **Color**
- **Oils and Acrylics**
- **Watercolor Paper**
- **Pen & Ink**
- **Pastels**
- **Colored Pencils**
- **Conte Crayons**
- **Charcoal**

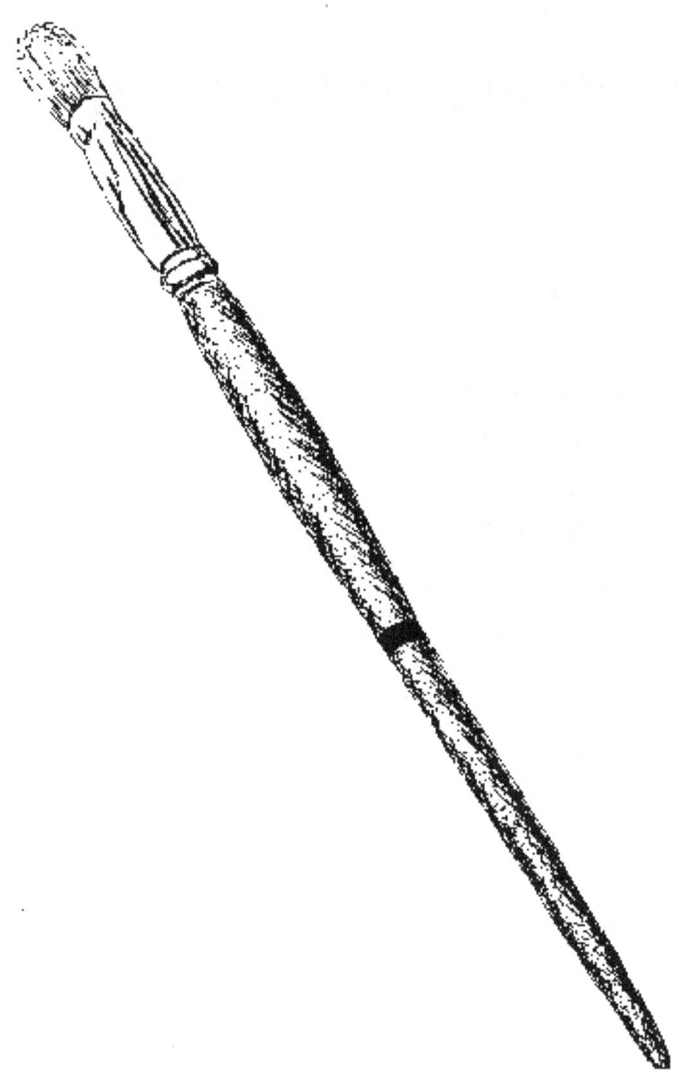

Filbert Brush

Watercolor

I paint mostly with watercolor. I have tried other media. I fully intend to paint more water miscible (mixable) oils in the future, but watercolor is very seductive. It has a lot of advantages. It dries quickly and is easy to transport. I can layer watercolor washes and glazes as soon as one layer is dry, or paint wet on wet and let the colors blend magically the way watercolors do. Watercolors take up less room than canvases and dry in minutes compared to oils that take months to dry.

Begin by buying watercolor paint in tubes. Squeeze some of each color into the pans in the palette box. Leave the lid open and let them dry for a week. When you are ready to paint, dip a brush in water and then into the dried paint. Mix the water and paint in the mixing area of the palette box. Add more water and additional colors till you get the exact shade you want. A metal palette box is a good investment. It has room for holding and mixing paints, and it travels well. Artists sometimes complain of mold on their paints. I have never had that problem, probably because I let the paints dry out well, and possibly because I use distilled water for painting.

Work on a flat surface. Brush a little water on a small section of the drawing. After the shine of the water has "flashed off," dip a wet, round watercolor brush in watercolor paint, touch it to a piece of scrap watercolor paper to get rid of excess water, and paint. Be careful not to paint with a bead of water on the ferule of the brush. It could run down the brush and put too much water on the paper. Change the water often so it is always clean. Dirty water will adversely affect the painting. It might not ruin it, but it will take the crispness out of the lighter, brighter colors. Try adding a second or third color to the wet area of the paper and let the paint move freely. If you paint on paper that has a very wet spot on it, before the shine has flashed off, something called a "bloom" can appear. It's a wet spot with paint that dries with a hard edge around it. On furniture it's a coffee ring. On clothing, it's a spot you would have dry cleaned. On a watercolor painting the best way to prevent bloom, while it is wet, is to squeeze water from a large round brush, splay the bristles, and let them absorb the excess water. Rinse the brush and repeat the process. If the paper has dried with a bloom on it, brush a small amount of water on the hard edge, dampen a wedge brush and carefully scrub it out. Blot it with a paper towel and repeat the process till the hard edge is no longer noticeable.

Often watercolor painting is more about fixing mistakes than painting. A wedge brush comes in handy for scrubbing out any paint that has dried where it shouldn't have. The wedge brush has a flat ferule, short bristles, and is cut on the diagonal. The one quarter inch size works well for gently scrubbing out unwanted edges.

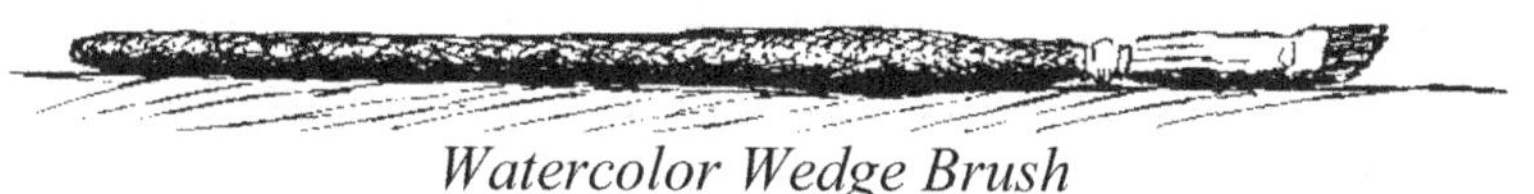

Watercolor Wedge Brush

There are other brushes one might find useful. A filbert brush has soft hair and rounded corners. It is good for painting between lines on French mats and probably has other uses that I haven't figured out yet. Some watercolor painters, usually those who teach workshops and want to get a painting done quickly for a class demo, use long handled brushes with flat ferules and fine bristles generally preferred by acrylic painters.

Most watercolor painters use "round" brushes. Buy sizes 4,6, and 10 or 12 to start, and trust me on this, you will never need a fan brush as long as you live. When a wider brush is required for applying a wash over a large area, choose a brush, about one inch across, made of soft sable or squirrel hair. I used a two inch brush from a paint store once, thinking that it would work just as well, and be cheaper than a same size artist's brush. It was a big mistake. The edge of the house painter's brush made nasty scratches on my paper. Its bristles were designed for use with house paint that is thicker and requires a stronger brush. The scratches could not be repaired.

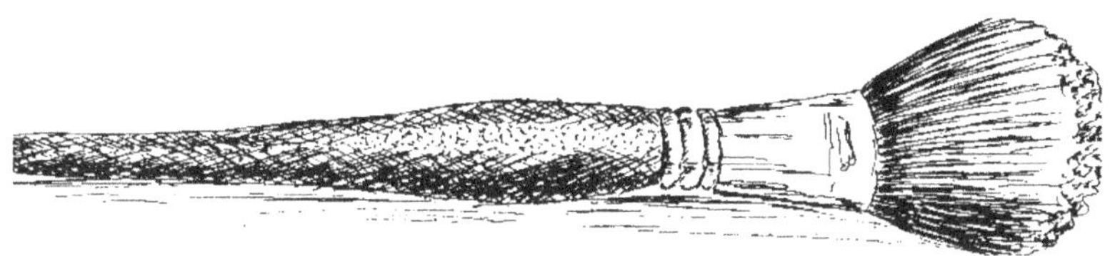

Watercolor Wash Brush

Good brushes enable you to paint neater edges, have better control, and result in more successful painting efforts than do cheap ones. An art store should let you dip a brush in water to see if it will form a nice point. Most stores will have a container of water near the brush display for this purpose. You'll need only a few brushes, but make sure they are of reasonably decent quality.

Some watercolor painters fail to brush clear water on each object or section they are painting before applying color. Watercolor paint, when laid down without a moist layer of clear water underneath, produces a dry, harsh looking, result. The luminosity of the paper does not come through. Always paint over a moist layer of clear water after the shine has "flashed off" unless you are painting very small, fine details or applying a glaze. You will notice that I often mention brushing clear water on a segment of a drawing, and letting it "flash off" before applying watercolor paint. Flashing off is a term that means letting it dry just until the shine of the water disappears. This is a very important technique. I cannot emphasize it enough in watercolor painting. I have seen artists who put forth great effort, enthusiasm and heart into their paintings, but who fail to do this. They might as well use full strength oil or acrylic instead of watercolor. Watercolor painted directly on dry paper produces a dull, overworked appearance. If the artist uses watercolor paint right out of the tube, it becomes even worse. Someday all that dried, thick, watercolor will end up as dust at the bottom of the frame, leaving the painting ready for the trash bin.

There are many techniques for enhancing watercolor paintings. Sometimes a little planned chaos works well. Sprinkle kosher salt on wet watercolor paint or lay wrinkled plastic wrap over it. Let it dry. Some artists begin by lightly spraying water on watercolor paper with a small beautician's size spray bottle for its finer mist. They splatter medium to dark colored watercolor paint on the paper randomly with a toothbrush dipped in diluted watercolor. Do this by holding the brush with bristles up and pulling back across it with your thumb or forefinger. Move the paper and let the color run. Use paper towels, not Kleenex®, to pick up the excess water.

You may hear the terms "wash" and "glaze" pertaining to watercolor. Here's how to do a wash for a sky. Apply clean water to the sky area with a wide brush. When the shine flashes off, and the paper is still moist, add horizontal streaks of sky colors such as blue, purple, and orange, etc. Tilt the paper sideways so streaks of color run horizontally. Tilting the paper vertically will make it look like it is raining. A glaze is a very sheer color, mixed with lots of water so the color is very light. It is applied without putting clear water on the previously painted area in order to avoid disturbing the paint. You might want to apply a green glaze over a tree trunk to indicate moss, or a pale purple glaze over a yellow stucco building to dull down the color. It is important to understand the difference between a wash and a glaze. Both techniques are useful.

Any painting and drawing experience will be valuable as you move from one medium to another. Some people say that if you can paint good watercolors, you will be able to paint good oil paintings. They suggest that it is harder to achieve similar results if you paint oils before you learn to paint watercolors. The idea is that if you are used to producing pleasing, though accidental, effects in watercolor, you might work harder to achieve similar results with oils. Don't be afraid to make large watercolor paintings to give the beauty of the water room to show up. In fact, the larger they are, the better. Paint small oil paintings, if you wish, because oil stays put and does not blend and swirl like watercolor. Feel free to experiment with various painting media for the experience will add to your knowledge, enjoyment and fulfillment as an artist.

After finishing a watercolor painting, be sure to spray its back and front with a fixative to lessen the danger of mold, mildew, and insect damage. Do this outside and wear a respirator to avoid breathing the spray.

Color

Oil painters are sometimes taught to paint two pictures of the same scene. The first one, a "grisaille" painting done in shades of gray, helps the artist figure out where the darks and lights should be. Once the grisaille is done the painter does a second, identical painting, in color. Most of us don't have time for this. So, unless you plan to paint all your pictures in shades of gray, you will need to know something about color.

James McNeill Whistler's famous "Study in Gray and Black" otherwise known as "Whistler's Mother," is all in gray tones. I had seen it many times in books and magazines and always thought it was a small painting until I saw it at the Musee d'Orsay in Paris. The painting is large, close to life sized. Incidentally, European museums were decidedly not handicapped accessible when I was there in 1998. At the Musee d'Orsay, people were carrying baby strollers up two long flights of stairs, then riding several escalators to get to the Impressionist paintings. The only visible elevator was a freight elevator with a big sign in French stating that it was not available to the public. But I digress. At any rate, Whistler's Mother must have made a wonderful thumbnail sketch because it reduces down in size very nicely. At the Musee d'Orsay it was exhibited with a colorful riot of Impressionist paintings. It looked almost as if they didn't have a category for paintings in gray, and instead, put it in with painters from the same time period.

Drying can affect paint color. Look at your paintings after they have dried completely. They may need some color adjustments. Acrylic colors dry darker than they are painted. Watercolors dry lighter. Some people say oils dry darker, while others say they don't. At any rate, oils do not dry lighter than they are painted. Drying affects the intensity of paint colors.

Complementary colors are an integral part of any discussion about color. Every color has a complement. The complement is the color opposite another on the color wheel. Buy a color wheel at any art supply store. One of my watercolor paintings included a beeswax candle. I painted it in Naples yellow and was quite happy with it until I added a shadow of pale Payne's gray on the left side of the candle. It looked dull and uninteresting. Then I remembered that the complement of yellow is purple. I glazed a little Dioxazine Violet over the Payne's gray, and it made an enormous difference. Instead of being a pale yellow candle with a boring, flat shadow, the candle and its shadow suddenly had warmth and appeal. Yellow and purple are complements.

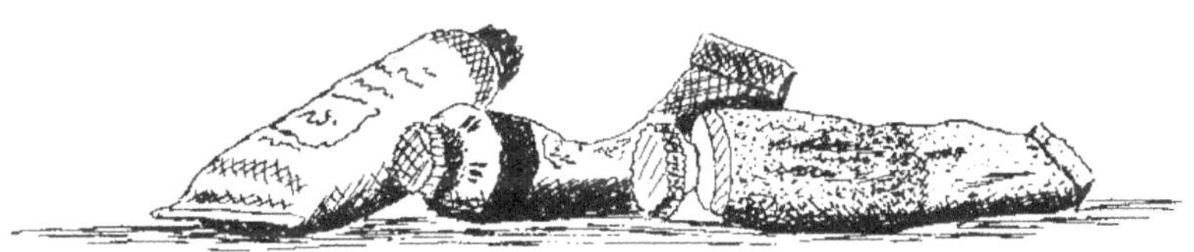

Watercolor Paint in Tubes

When painting trees with green leaves, either deciduous or coniferous, brighten or darken the greens with some yellow or blue. Gray or reduce the intensity of green by adding some red tones. When painting grass on a lawn, streak in some Indian red when the green is almost dry and it will look right. To paint a bluish green evergreen tree, add dark red here and there. Red and green are complements. The greens in nature are usually more subdued than the color that comes right out of the paint tube and generally require that you mix colors to get the desired shade.

Orange and blue are complements. Paint a blue sea with a boat and a touch of orange on a flag or life preserver and the whole scene will perk up. Add some orange to the blue water to tone down the blue. Sometimes a tiny bit of the bright complementary color is all that is necessary. Too much can be overpowering. Don't be afraid to play with and think about colors. Paint a brown horse but let a viewer, who gets close to it, find streaks of blue and orange on it somewhere. Another painting might be best painted with a limited palette of shades of one color and its complement. Still another might look right done in the primary colors red, blue, yellow with green, orange, purple, and black and white added. Thinking about color choices will cause you to make conscious decisions about color and your paintings will benefit from the process.

Colors have value, which is their lightness or darkness, and hue, which is their variety or tint. For me, one of the easiest ways to study color is to look at mass produced clothing groups. This is because I had a career as a retail fashion buyer for many years. Clothing manufacturers rely on elaborate color work done several years in advance by companies that analyze and plan fashion trend colors and coordinate them with other industries. If you wanted to match a red raincoat with a red car and a red sofa you could probably do it without much trouble. Being able to find products in matching colors in unrelated industries is not a coincidence. Study printed clothing, too, and notice how some colors are combined with others. Dusty tones work well together. Bright primary colors and white do the same thing, as do groups of pastel colors. Earth tones work nicely with beige. You can get really bogged down analyzing whether one color is the same value or hue as the next. Pick up a clothing catalogue and look at the colors available for each item. Sometimes more than one color group is available as seasons change. Observe clothing carefully where the manufacturers have already done the color work for you. You will begin to recognize instinctively which colors work well together and which ones don't and it will influence your painting in a good way.

Sometimes a new artist will think "My work isn't worth anything, so I might as well buy cheap paints, paper, brushes, etc., because they will work just fine while I am learning to paint." He or she may paint a great looking picture only to see it fade in a few years and lose its appeal. Artists' quality paints reputedly keep their original color better than student grade products. Test them yourself. I have found that even one or two colors of some brands of artists' grade watercolors will fade. Naples yellow and sap green come to mind. Paint a brush stroke of each color in your palette on a piece of paper and tape it, face out, to the inside of a south window for a few weeks. Keep a list in pencil on the back with each color listed in the order you have arranged them on the front. After some time passes you will have a good idea which colors will keep their intensity. It may be worthwhile to buy artists' quality products from the beginning.

Oils and Acrylics

The classic way to begin an oil painting is to draw a picture with vine charcoal on gesso primed canvas. Make corrections by erasing the charcoal with a kneaded eraser. When the drawing looks right, take it outside and spray it with a workable fixative. Be sure the word "workable" is on the label. If you fail to spray the drawing, the charcoal will mix with and smudge the paint. Protect yourself by wearing a respirator while you spray the work. Some artists skip the charcoal and draw with paint. Most oil painters paint dark to light and fat over lean. Paint dark or shadowed areas first with the complement of the color you intend to use later. Make the paint quite thin in the beginning. Gradually build it up so that the layers you paint last are the thickest paint. You might choose to paint "alla prima" and do the painting all at once with wet paint on wet paint. Either way you'll need only two or three brushes in different sizes.

Winston Churchill (1871-1947) began oil painting when he was forty under the pseudonym, Charles Morin. In 1927 an English painter, Walter R. Sickert, (1860-1942) wrote to him as requested, with advice on how to paint in oil. Sickert, who had been influenced by James McNeill Whistler (1843-1903) and Edgar Degas, (1834-1917) advised Churchill to mix up three light colored batches of ultramarine blue and white artists' oil paint in small bowls. The first mixture was to be very light, the second medium, and the third a little darker, but all were to be fairly light in color. He suggested mixing each batch with equal parts of linseed oil and turpentine with a palette knife until the paints would "run freely off the knife." He told Churchill to brush the second shade of paint over the entire canvas, and then paint the design using the lighter and darker tones. Churchill would continue painting, adding other colors as needed until the painting gradually took shape, letting each layer dry thoroughly before adding the next. Sickert believed that painting with a brush instead of a palette knife gave added tooth to the previous layers of paint by creating an irregular surface so that subsequent layers would hold the paint well. [Ref. 1, pp. 62-64]

I saw an original Churchill painting in England at Lord Ismay's (who was Churchill's chief of staff) grandson's home which was part of a Tauck.com tour. The painting was dark and dreary and probably one of his early attempts. Even though the painting was dark, Churchill did not use black paint. He preferred "Neutral Tint" (a Winsor and Newton color similar to Payne's gray) instead. Churchill used everything he could to assist him in his painting including a grid system for transfering photos to canvas. He also used slides projected onto canvas because he felt that since he was starting to paint at forty, he was too old to waste time learning to draw well. [Ref. 1, p. 72]

When I experimented with water miscible (mixable) oils they seemed a bit stiff to work with right out of the tube and too thin when I added water. A friend recommended using a drop or two of a linseed oil product called Max Medium that is designed for use with them. I haven't tried it yet, but have been told it works very well. Using water-miscible oils eliminates the need for bad smelling, and probably toxic, turpentine.

Brush strokes or palette knife marks should not draw one's eye to them. They should be uniformly consistent. Distinctive brush strokes, such as those made by van Gogh, Seurat, and Monet, and others, will give you an idea of their importance. Van Gogh's brush strokes are bold but uniform. A van Gogh brush stroke on a Renoir painting, however, would not look right. You'd notice it right away. Brush strokes should be consistent within the work. I saw paintings in an art magazine with brush strokes as lines that went around each figure. The artist had not taken the time to pull the paint away from them. This was not done anywhere else in the painting. It really looked quite bad. A couple of months later the same magazine had an article about brush strokes.

Oil paintings are usually varnished and not placed under glass. A valuable painting might, however, be placed under tempered glass, for protection against vandalism, separated from it by spacers. Be sure the painting has dried completely, six months to a year, before you varnish it. If you brush varnish on an oil painting before the paint is dry, the paint will streak. There are spray varnishes that eliminate this problem, but the painting should still be dry when you apply the varnish, because if it isn't, it will crack when the paint finally dries. If you spray the painting with a retouch varnish before it has dried for the requisite amount of time, you should still varnish it when it has finished drying.

Acrylic paints dry quickly and thin and clean up with water. Squeeze acrylic paints from tubes onto a glass plate or wax paper palette. Save the paints for another day by covering them with plastic wrap. Unlike oils, certain combinations of acrylic colors turn muddy gray when mixed together. Some oil painters first draw on canvas with acrylic paint. Sources disagree as to whether this will hold up over time. It might be acceptable considering the fact that acrylic gesso is used as a primer on most, if not all, primed canvas being sold today. Wet oil and acrylic paints should never be mixed together because their drying times differ.

Watercolor Paper

Watercolor paper comes in different weights as well as hot press, cold press, and rough texture. All work well for watercolor painting. Many watercolorists favor cold press, 140 pound paper. (A stack of this paper one meter high weighs 140 pounds.) The lighter weights tend to buckle as they are painted.

There are several ways to flatten paper before or after it buckles. One way is to tape all four sides down to a rigid support such as plexiglass. Three hundred pound paper does not require taping down. That's what I usually use, but I have found some papers between 140 and 300 pounds that are very nice. "Armatruda" is a pretty paper, made in Italy, with four deckled edges. "Aquarelle," a handmade paper by Moulin de Larroque, a French company, is heavy, rough, and nice when you want to let white flecks of paper show. These papers are available in art supply catalogues.

If paper of any weight is not flat after a watercolor painting has dried, flatten it by placing it between clean sheets of watercolor paper and piling heavy books on top of it. In a week or two it will be flat. A friend of mine sprays water on the backs of watercolor paintings and irons them flat. She uses brown craft paper between the front of the painting and the ironing board, and irons the back. I haven't tried it, but she says it works. Changes in humidity can cause changes in the paper and some slight rippling should not be considered a defect. Acid free, rag paper will stay nice forever provided you keep acidic papers and wood from touching it. Good paper with proper sizing allows you to scrub out mistakes without ruining the paper's finish or putting holes in it.

Blocks of watercolor paper contain sheets like a tablet, except that instead of being bound on one side, all four sides are bound. An inch or so is left unbound so a razor blade can be inserted and pushed around all the sides to remove the top sheet after a painting has been completed and has dried.

Be wary of paper made of plastic components. I heard about four ladies from Greensburg, PA, who went painting one very hot summer day. They were trying out a new type of plastic based paper. They painted on it all day with their watercolors, then stood the paintings up in the back seat of their vehicle for the ride home. By the time they got there, all the paint had slid to the bottom of their paintings. Paper needs to have some tooth and absorbency to hold watercolor and as well as other painting media.

Sometimes it's fun to paint on Japanese masa paper pasted to watercolor paper. Tape the edges of a 22 x 30 inch (full sheet) of watercolor paper to a firm support with masking tape. The support should be something that won't absorb water or be hurt by having water on it overnight, such as a laminated countertop or a large piece of plexiglass a little larger than the paper. Mix one level tablespoon of dry wallpaper paste and nine tablespoons of water together with a small whisk. Set it aside. Pencil a small "X" on each corner of the rough side of the masa paper. Gently wad the masa paper into a ball and place it in a bowl of water for four or five minutes. Meanwhile, spread the paste onto the taped down watercolor paper. The water should be getting into the creases of the masa by this time. If it becomes too wet, it will rip. Carefully remove it from the water, unfold it, and lay it on the pasted paper with the "X" side up. Brush outwards gently from the center with a wallpaper brush. Try to get the air bubbles out without ripping the delicate paper. Let it dry thoroughly. It may take a day or two. If the full sheet is larger than you need, cut it to size with scissors after it has completely dried.

When the paper is dry, paint on it almost the way you would on regular watercolor paper, but don't use masking fluid to block out areas you want to keep white. If you do, the sheer masa may tear off with the masking when you try to remove it. When you paint on masa paper, colors will leach into the wrinkles. This is part of the paper's charm, and looks great if the color is where you want it to be, but it can be a problem if a dark color leaches into a light colored area. Avoid this by keeping the brush as dry as possible, while having some paint on it, where a dark area meets a light area. Unlike painting on regular watercolor paper, do not wet the areas you are painting with clear water before you apply color unless you are sure that color leaching into adjacent areas will not be a problem. When the painting is completely dry. Spray fix both sides outside while wearing a respirator.

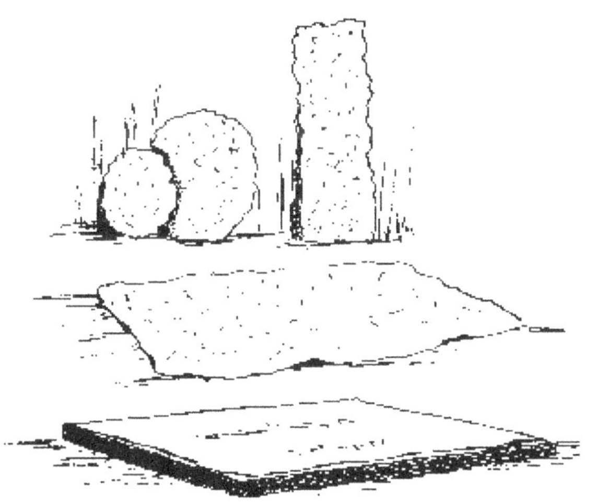

Assorted Watercolor Papers

Pen and Ink

My initial work with pen and ink came about when a local charity needed some art for a cookbook fundraiser project. See part of it at geocities.com/recipeswithhistory. The objective is not to blacken whole areas with solid color. For some reason it is difficult for commercial printers to print solid areas of black color without leaving gaps or blobs. Printers often have written directions that explain this for particular projects. Most pen and ink drawing is done with small straight lines called hatching, or straight lines "X"ed over other straight lines called cross hatching, or little pointillist dots, or simple lines, hence the name: "line art." Pen and ink allows the artist to indicate shadow and form with a variety of pleasing marks. Most of the illustrations in this book are pen and ink drawings.

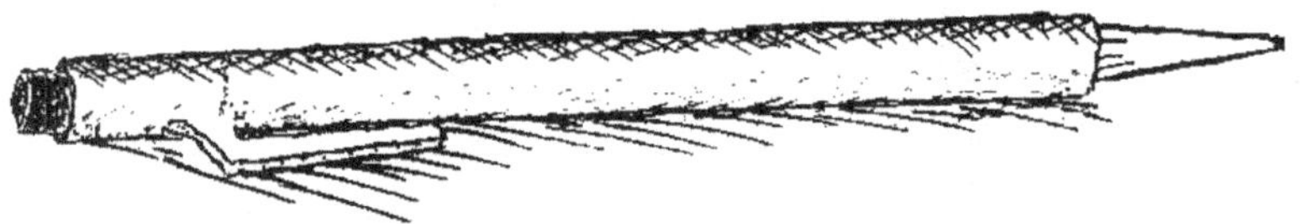

My Favorite Sharpwriter® Pencil

The easy way to get a pen and ink drawing to come out right is to draw lightly first in pencil on Bristol board tablet paper. Make the drawing a little larger than you need it to be when published. Pencil allows you to fix mistakes and get it right before using ink. The more you draw, the more you will use short, sketchy lines instead of trying to draw the proverbial "straight line." If a line appears to be going in the wrong direction, all you have to do is correct the direction with the next short, sketchy line. When the drawing is the way you want it, go over the pencil lines with pen and ink.

The pen used for line art is called a crow quill pen. Some pens, like your favorite Sharpie® might seem perfect for this, but they aren't. The lines drawn with a crow quill pen will look fine and genteel. It is the modern equivalent of a crow feather. Some art supply catalogues sell the crow quill pen points (nibs) and pen handles separately. Art stores sell them in a package called a sketching project set. Use a medium sized nib if you are planning to reduce the size of the drawing for printing.

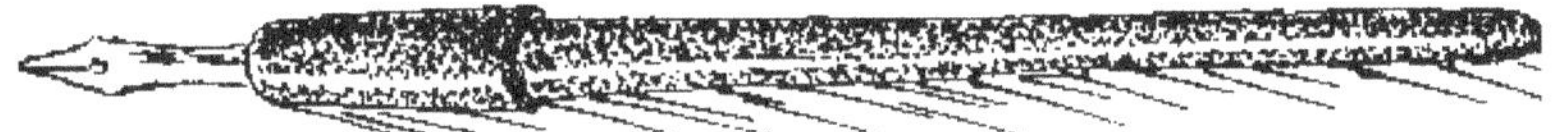

Crow Quill Pen

If you plan to paint watercolor over an ink drawing, use India Ink which is a waterproof drawing ink. Otherwise use non water-proof drawing ink. Both come in small bottles. The water-proof ink cleans up with turpentine. Non waterproof ink washes off with water. Touch only the upper part of the pen. When dipping the pen in ink, the lower part of the pen will get ink on it from touching the jar. As with a paint brush, holding the pen above the ferule will provide more control. Every time you dip the pen in the ink jar, use a piece of Kleenex® to touch the rounded part of the nib until there is no ink filling the little round hole on top, otherwise excess ink may fall on the paper. Kleenex® works better than a paper towel for this. Let the ink dry thoroughly, preferably overnight. Then go over the whole drawing with a kneaded eraser. This will remove all the pencil lines and brighten it up. I saw the cartoonist, Al Hirschfeld, (1903-2003) do this on TV when he was explaining to an interviewer how he did his drawings. My art teacher told me the same thing later. Working in pencil first saves an amazing amount of time, paper and anguish.

If you are saving art to a disk, scan the original art. Unless you own software that will allow you to scan and piece together large artwork in sections, the drawing should fit on the scanner bed. Saving it at 200 dpi (dots per square inch) will save a huge amount of space in the file, as will reducing the size by a percentage or inches before sending it to the paint feature. Some projects require art scanned from 200 to 600 dpi. Kinko's® can help you with 600dpi scanning if the work is small enough to fit on their scanner bed. Check the job specifications before you do the pen and ink drawing project.

For camera-ready art, reduce each original on a photocopier to the required size. Cut out the copies while leaving some space around them. Use a photo blue pencil to mark exactly where you plan to place each one on the camera ready laser (not inkjet) printed page. Have a re-stickable glue stick (Staples® sells the 3M Scotch® brand ones that I use.) and a roll of wax paper handy. Use a new piece of wax paper for each drawing. Hold the corner of the back of the photocopied drawing down with your thumb and pull the glue stick away from it as you go across it. Make sure the back of the drawing, including the edges, is completely covered with one or two strokes of the glue. Position the photocopy on the page within the photo blue pencil marks. Later, if you decide you want a different piece of art in that spot, carefully peel off the first drawing and paste on a new one. Restickable glue sticks are not as messy as permanent glue sticks. They seem to have been made with the artist in mind. Note that ink jet printing does not reproduce well. The edges look a little fuzzy. This is why camera ready art is best reduced on a photocopier instead of being reduced on a scanner and printed with an ink jet printer.

Although you may choose to reduce drawings for camera-ready printing, be careful not to make the original art too large. I drew what I considered a great looking ear of corn for the fundraiser cookbook. The ear was horizontal and the cookbook was taller than it was wide. When I reduced the drawing on a photocopier to the required camera-ready size, some areas came out too light. I had to go back to the drawing and darken parts of it. Try to make drawings no more than double the size required. The copier I used would not reduce more than fifty percent so I had to reduce the copy to get it to the right size. It worked, but it took more time and effort than it should have, and the result was a copy of a copy.

Pastels

Pastels are pieces of colored chalk designed to adhere to "pastel" paper which is available in many colors. Colored paper helps to unify the painting. (Oil pastels are different and work more like oil paint.) Pastel paintings can be done quickly because there is no drying time. Pastels can be blended with your fingers, drawn with short uniform strokes in one direction, cross hatched, or held sideways for a wide color stroke. Use pastels on an easel so the dust will fall down and away from you. Don't blow the dust away. A HEPA filter might be a good investment. Draw and add details later with a pastel pencil.

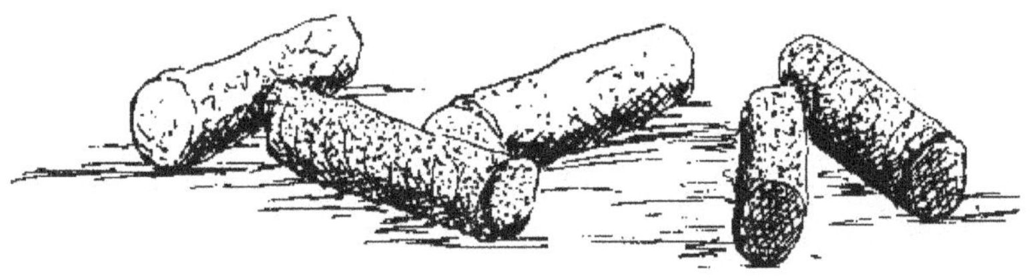

Soft Pastels

Make a drawing and use yellow or other pale colors to exaggerate areas that will be light. Apply very dark colors to exaggerate areas that you plan to leave dark. Stay within the lines of the drawing, continuing with colors that are not as light and not as dark as those applied first, and blend them with your fingers or Q tips. Use pale shades of pastel for the final light areas but avoid the chalky appearance of pure white for skin tones. Let a dot of white indicate the reflected light on an eye. Create uniformity by using most colors in several places in the painting.

Pastel consistency varies from soft to hard. Use the hard ones first and follow with soft pastels. The "tooth" in the paper is what holds pastels to it. As you apply more layers, the quality of the tooth lessens, and the pastel will be less likely to adhere properly.

Some artists spray each layer with a fixative designed for pastels. Some do not spray the last layer of pastel. The fixative changes the color intensity. Some artists don't use fixatives at all. To see some really fine pastel work, go to www.swannportraits.com and see the work of pastel artist Christine Swann.

Be careful when reframing a pastel painting. Too much moving and jarring can cause some of the pastel to come loose. Since pastel dust will always settle to the bottom of the picture, be sure to use a spacer between the mat and the painting or the colorful particles will adhere to the beveled edge of the mat and will detract from the appearance of the piece. Always use glass, not plexiglass when glazing pastels because static electricity in plexiglass will often cause pastel particles to gravitate to it.

Colored Pencils

Using a light touch, draw your design with colored pencils instead of regular graphite pencils. Graphite has an unfortunate tendency to be noticeable when used with colored pencils. Sharpen all the colored pencils and rub all the points against the cardboard back of the drawing paper tablet to wear each one down to a wide flat surface. Each pencil should glide over the paper allowing its texture to show through. When a colored pencil begins to make a crisp line instead of a soft, wide mark, rub it against the cardboard again to smooth and flatten it. I prefer Berol Prismacolor® colored pencils. Make smooth strokes across the paper so the tooth of the paper grabs the color as you move the pencil. Build up layers of complementary colors as well as the color you want to see when it's done. If you are painting a brown jug, you might want to use layers of brown, blue, and orange. It is sometimes possible to lay on as many as twelve colors. Add highlights of yellow or white last. Some colors, especially yellow, seem to contain more wax than others and this makes it harder for other colors to adhere to them.

Gain knowledge about mixing colors in other media by first experimenting with colored pencils. As you see how colors blend when you layer them over each other, you will begin to understand the ones that work well together and those that don't. Once you understand that blues don't stay blue when you layer them with yellow, you will be well on your way to understanding how to blend colors to achieve the shades you want in most media.

Conte Crayons

Conte crayons are hard little sticks of color, usually rust, white, black, reddish brown and brown with names like Sanguine and Bistre. Delightful drawings result from combining their muted colors with the colored paper designed for their use. As with pastels, the color of the paper unifies the drawing. The subdued shades of just a few Conte crayons on colored paper can produce a very nice piece of art.

A friend of mine says she achieves better control with Conte pencils than with Conte crayons. Conte crayons and pencils are nice to use if you take a figure drawing class. The colorful drawing is more interesting than one done in plain charcoal.

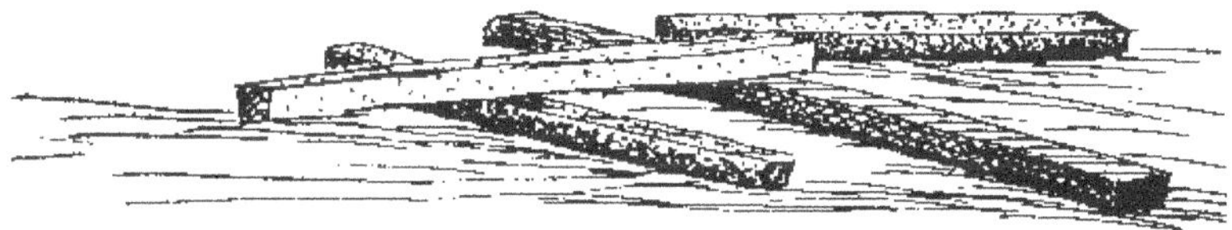

Conte Crayons

As with charcoal and pastels, hold the Conte crayon sideways and move it over the paper to shade a large area. It will leave a soft, wide layer of color and you will see the texture of the paper. Create highlights by erasing with a kneaded eraser. A highlight is light reflecting on a curve. If you need lines, use the crayon like a pencil to draw them. When you have finished, spray fix both sides of the page with a fixative.

Charcoal

Charcoal was the first medium I used when I began to study art at the age of forty-four. My art teacher began by teaching me to see dark and light areas in objects. I shaded and drew using pieces of vine charcoal. My first drawing was a single candle in a small, dish type candlestick. I learned to make it look rounded by putting in highlights, to measure in from the sides of the paper so the candle would stand straight up without leaning to one side or the other, and to ground the work by drawing lines at the base of the candle holder which made it look like it was resting on a table.

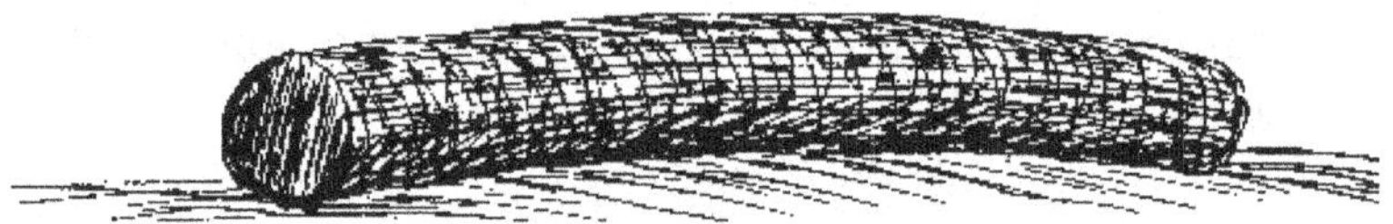

Vine Charcoal

Lightly shade a broad section with the side of the charcoal stick. Draw a line with the point. If you get too much charcoal on the drawing paper, a kneaded eraser will remove it easily. Charcoal pencils are harder than vine charcoal, produce finer lines, and can be used with Conte crayons. Vine charcoal comes in varying thicknesses and the pieces curve like a vine. To blend charcoal on the paper, use a Q-tip or pieces of paper felt rolled up to a point called blending tortillions. Blending charcoal with your fingers will leave them extremely dirty. When finished, spray the drawing with a fixative or the charcoal will rub off on everything it touches and the drawing will lose its sharpness.

Problem Solving

- **The Painting Process**
- **Transposing Images to Painting Surfaces**
- **Measuring and Positioning**
- **Negative Space**
- **Composition**
- **Perspective**
  - **People in Paintings**
  - **The Checkerboard**
  - **Interior Perspective**
  - **Drawing Round Vases and Tables**
  - **Roof Peaks**
  - **Basic House**
  - **Row Houses**
  - **Roofs on Row Houses**
  - **Barn Roofs**
  - **Pennsylvania Bank Barn**
  - **Buildings on a Hillside**
  - **Perspective from Above**

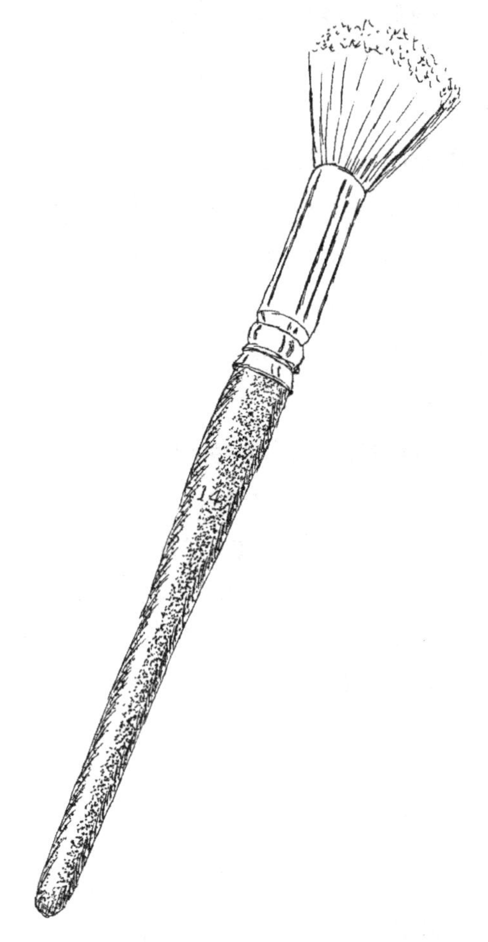

Round Mop Brush for Watercolor Painting

The Painting Process

When I have finished my drawing and have started to paint with watercolor or oil, I sometimes begin to panic. Perhaps the painting isn't progressing the way I envisioned; the colors are wrong, or something else doesn't look right. When that happens, I am sometimes tempted to give up on it, paint over it, or throw it away. I have learned, however, that a painting at the panic point can still become a good one. To ensure that it does, there are several things one can do. Get some distance from the work. Put it across the room and look at it while you work out on an exercise machine. After half an hour you may realize what the painting needs. Make a list of the problems. Analyze them and figure out how to fix them.

Ask yourself some questions. Are the dark areas dark enough? Are the shadows right? Does a color, a hard edge, lack of an edge or an odd brush stroke annoy you? Are objects blending into each other? Do they require more definition? Is your eye drawn to some minor flaw that competes with the focal point of the work? Think of the painting you envisioned in your mind's eye before you began to paint. Ask yourself where the work strays from your original plan, or what could you add to make it more interesting. Indicate human presence with a pot of flowers, tools, toys, a mailbox, or whatever is appropriate for the work. Try adding a bird, a dog, or a person to a landscape. Add a few acorns, chestnuts, berries, flowers or petals to a still life. Keep working on the painting. When you are satisfied with its appearance from a distance, look at it closely and repair any small defects. Look at the painting again from a distance and, if you are satisfied, call it finished.

Transposing Images to Painting Surfaces

Artists often paint using a photograph or drawing as a guide. Some draw a grid over the photo and then draw a corresponding one on the paper. The key is to have the same proportions in both. Put a center line on both the photo and the paper. Subdivide each several times. Hand copy each grid section from the drawing or photo to the corresponding grid on the paper, enlarging it as you go. If the proportion is not correct, you will end up with some very unnaturally sized elements.

Prior to making the grid, ensure that the proportion is correct by placing the photograph or sketch snugly in one corner of the paper or canvas. Place a yardstick across the diagonally opposite corners of the photo to the diagonally opposite corner of the painting surface.

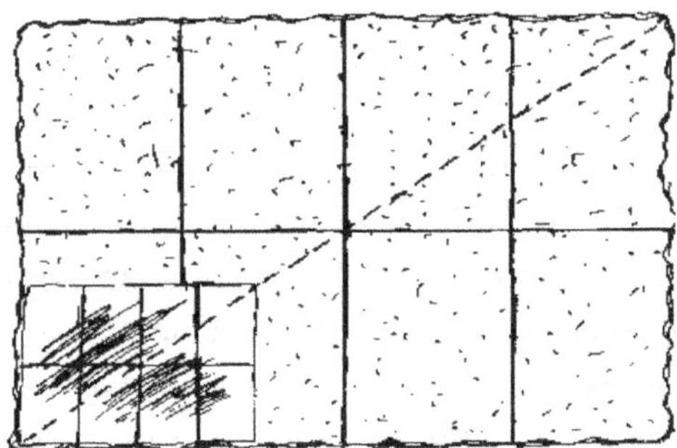

Make a grid and copy corresponding areas
that are proportionately correct.

If the yardstick goes above the diagonally opposite corner, cut off the right side of the paper at that point.

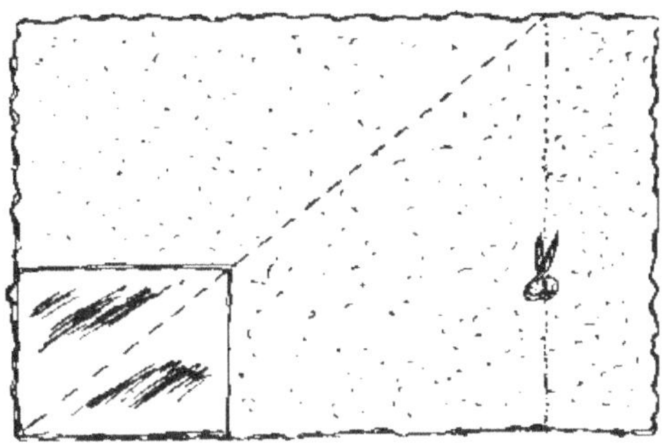

Transferring a photo or sketch to paper.
When the paper is too wide, cut off part of the paper.

If the yardstick goes below the diagonally opposite corner, cut off the top of the paper from that point. When you draw a grid, if you feel you need one, the proportions will be correct.

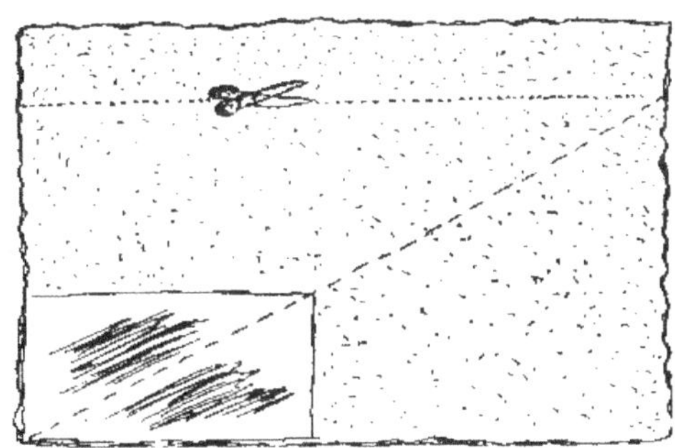

Transferring photo or sketch to paper.
When the paper is too high, cut off part of the paper.

You may want to crop the photograph or thumbnail sketch and leave the painting surface the size it already is. Place the yardstick diagonally across the canvas and crop the photo until its diagonal corners are under the yardstick. If using stretched canvas, this is the easiest way. Paper can be cut, so if you are planning to do a watercolor or drawing, it doesn't matter which way you make it work.

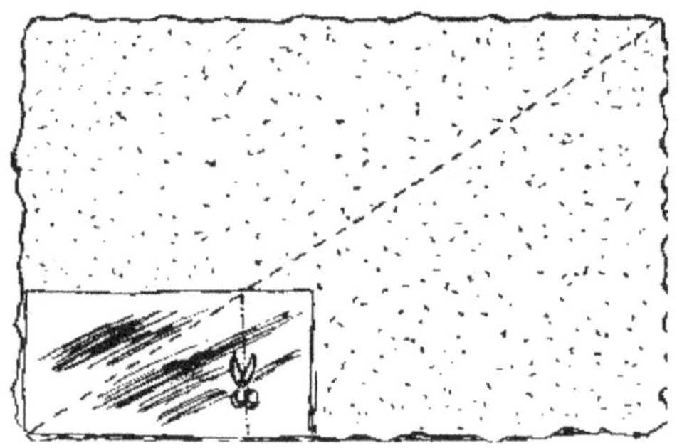

Transferring a photo or sketch to paper.
When the photo is too wide, cut off part of the side.

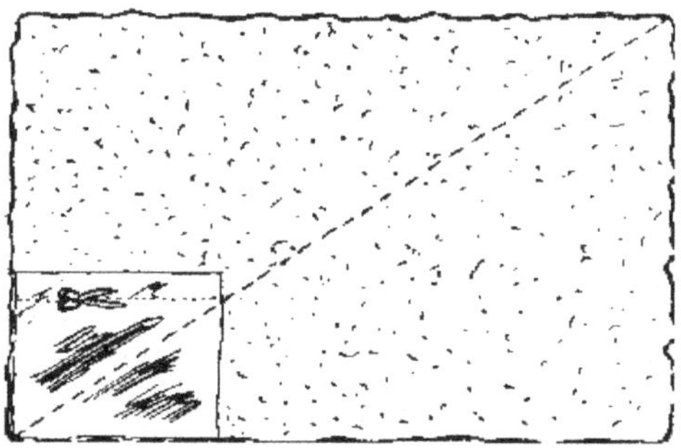

Transferring a photo or sketch to paper.
When the photo is too tall, cut off part of the top.

Measuring and Positioning

An amateur artist began to sketch a house. Unfortunately she started with the porch and by the time she got to the roof it was off the page. Let's suppose you want to paint a particular tree, gate, house, or still life. You may have done a thumbnail sketch and decided not to use a grid to transfer the scene to the painting surface. You know where the highest and lowest parts are located. Make a pencil mark on the painting surface to correspond with those parts. Do this for the width as well. It will prevent the drawing from taking on a life of its own and wandering all over the place. If there is a center point or item, indicate where you want that to be. In a still life, for example, if you are painting four jugs in a row, mark where the top of the largest one should be, where the first one starts and where the last one ends. If the smallest one is half the size of the largest one, make a mark to indicate where it should be.

If it helps, don't be afraid to use a ruler, but resist the temptation to draw straight lines with it. Instead, use the ruler as a guide and draw the lines free hand. The resulting art will be more natural looking. Learn to measure whatever you are painting or drawing against other items in your drawing. Do this with any subject matter. The small guide marks will help you figure out where each part belongs. If you notice where one object bumps up against another as you go along, your painting will develop in a very nice way and it will look right when it's finished.

Negative Space

The space between things is called negative space. It is quite possible to draw the negative space and end up with the objects themselves reasonably well defined. Just as a white flower may not be painted completely white, you might not draw its actual petal shapes at all. You may find it easier to paint the flower by filling in around its petals with background color. Its shape will begin to appear and it will give you confidence to finish painting it. Try this technique when copying a photograph you have taken. Turn it upside down and draw the negative space. Then turn the photo and the drawing right side up again and see how well you have drawn it. When you want to paint something complicated or difficult, seeing and drawing the shapes between and around the items in the composition will help you figure out where everything else belongs.

Composition

Most artists avoid placing either the focal point or the horizon in the exact center of a painting. Portrait subjects look better off center, too. Some artists think composition is most effective when large items are placed on the left side of the painting. Paint and draw so that the lines in the painting lead the viewer around it to discover its secrets. Landscapes are generally painted right up to the edges of the paper or canvas. Other subjects might not be. Flowers are often painted as botanicals in the center of the page. It is generally best to be consistent within your painting design. If you're painting an item that extends off the paper on the left, balance it by allowing part of it to lead out of the picture on the right. Consider similar treatment at the top and bottom of the painting. One of the easiest composition concepts to understand is the "S" or "Z" format. Both are essentially mirror images of each other. Lines should lead the viewer into the painting, through it, out of it, and back in again.

An example of the "S" format in a painting is the watercolor "Unexpected Guest" by Charles M. Russell. [Ref. 14, p.107] A mountain comes in from the right and slopes to the left. A closer hill comes in from the left and slopes to the right. A log and a sleeping cowboy provide a line from the upper right to the lower left. There is more to this painting, but its foundation is rock solid composition.

Common sense will tell you that a painting with "S" composition alone should have a few vertical lines somewhere to lead one's eyes up and down as well as back and forth across the painting. Russell understood this and added trees and a bear on its hind legs to the right of the trees. Balance any composition by making sure its skeleton of lines doesn't leave gaps and isn't monotonous.

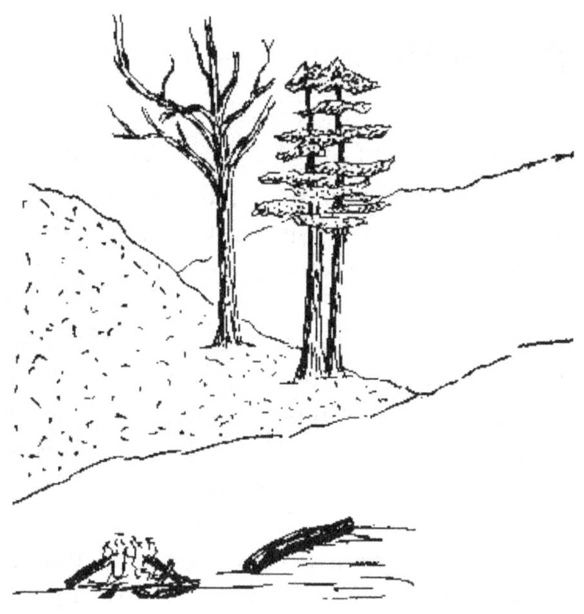

"S" or "Z" Composition with Vertical Elements.

There are more complicated composition theories that divide the painting surface into squares and triangles of varying sizes and specify where each belongs in the painting. Those theories are better studied in text books on the subject than in this guide. For our purposes just remember that lines in a painting should lead the viewer around and through it so that parts of it are not missed.

Perspective

A knowledge of perspective is helpful, whether for drawing and painting the ocean, trees, people, buildings, or even clouds. Perspective adds depth to paintings. It makes distant things look far away, and nearby things appear closer. It helps us figure out the placement of furniture in a room, how much table top to show, where to place peaks on a roof, how large to make people in a painting, and many other things. The term "vanishing point," is simply the point you see when staring at your own visual horizon. It can be at the bottom of the basement steps, straight down to earth from an airplane, or the horizon of the earth from where you stand. There can be more than one vanishing point on the horizon. Buildings usually have at least two, one relating to each of the two sides that are visible. One may be far off the painting surface. Objects appear bigger, as they get closer to the viewer, because they are farther away from the vanishing point. Note that when transferring architectural elements to paper from a photograph, the perspective may be off. You might need to go back and look at the scene, or determine your own vanishing points and make the elements function correctly with them.

People in Paintings

Make your paintings more interesting by including people or things that indicate their presence. We like to observe our fellow humans doing things and are drawn to paintings that show them at work or play. Furthermore, people using machinery or doing ordinary work may look more interesting a hundred years from now than they do today. As time passes, equipment and procedures change. A painting may become increasingly appealing because it shows people wearing old fashioned clothing, driving antique cars, or using simple household utensils that were current when the painting was made but which, over time, have become outdated.

Styles change. Hemlines, hats, and dresses all contribute to a modern effect today that may appear quaint in the future. A few years ago I worked on a series of paintings that related to the 1940's. I went to the library and found clothing details in a book that showed typical men's and women's clothing for every ten year period since the late 1800's. Fashion from any era is surprisingly easy to document. Most clothing in the twentieth century was factory made ready-to-wear as opposed to home made. Before mass produced clothing became dominant, women read about fashion and copied and sewed styles they saw in magazines. Accurate fashion information is available for any era that you might want to paint.

What about a person in a crowd or in the distance? How is the body proportioned? An adult head is about one-seventh of the total height. Children's heads may be one third to one sixth of their height. If there is no child handy to be measured, refer to pictures in catalogues that sell children's clothing. Artists often keep a file of people in various poses along with other possible painting subjects.

To draw an adult figure, mark the paper where the top of the head and the bottom of the feet should be. Measure this distance and divide it by seven. In the top one seventh, draw an oval shape for the head. Leave some space for the neck and sketch a rectangle below it to indicate the position of the torso. Connect it to the head with a neck. Add arms and legs and make the feet bigger than you are probably inclined to do.

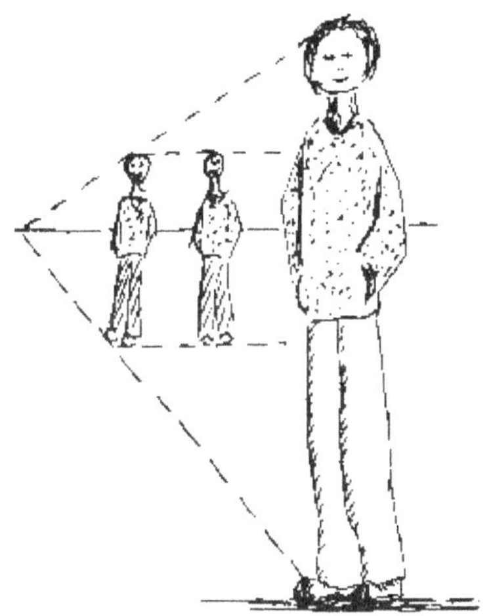

People in perspective

It helps to take a figure drawing class. If you have never painted before, note that a "life" drawing class is code for nude models. Some models bring really great props. I took a class once where the model showed up with a huge rubber ball. He posed with it on his back like Atlas, of Greek mythology, who held the world on his shoulders. Oh yes, not all the nude models are female!

To add more people in the distance, draw a line from the top of the head to a vanishing point on the horizon. How do you find that? Just pick a spot where you think the viewer's eye would be looking, and put it there. Draw a line to the same point from the bottom of the figure's feet. If you move the figures across the paper, let horizontal lines indicate the location of same size figures.

Some artists who put small figures of people in their paintings do not paint detailed faces. If people ask you why you haven't painted the faces, then paint the faces. If the face is very small you may need only a couple of gray dots for the eyes, the nose, and a small line to indicate where the lips meet. Blank faces containing no indications of eyes or other features sometimes draw one's attention to them. Any detail, or lack of one, that unintentionally attracts the eye of the viewer should be considered a defect that you ought to fix.

The Checkerboard

It is useful to know how to draw a checkerboard for reasons other than just for drawing checkerboards. You might want to draw a marble, parquet, or brick floor, banquet tables, or rows of glassware. The Dutch masters knew how to do the floors beautifully. The black and white marble tiles in their paintings recede neatly into the distance. This technique will help you do that.

I became interested in checkerboard perspective when I tried to paint a picture I titled "Red Square." A friend had visited eastern Europe and had brought me a set of nested Russian dolls. The Soviet Union had just collapsed and I wanted to do a painting with the dolls in a row, standing on a checkerboard, with black and white squares everywhere except for one red square in the front left corner. I tried it in colored pencil. Some rows of the checker board seemed to flip up at me. They did not recede correctly. I began to read about perspective, and figured out how to make the painting work. I drew it again and painted it in watercolor. Finally, it was right.

Toward the upper center of the paper, put a small "X" to indicate the vanishing point. The vanishing point could be in places other than the center. For the checkerboard, mark off eight equal spaces along the bottom edge of the paper. Somewhere between the bottom of the page and the vanishing point, draw a horizontal line across the paper. If you were drawing a room's interior, this would be where the floor meets the wall. Using a ruler, with the edge touching both the vanishing point and each of the equally spaced marks, draw lines from the bottom of the page to the horizontal line.

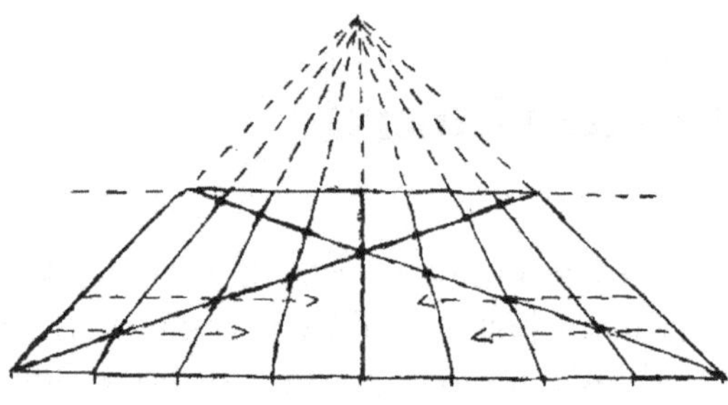

How to begin drawing a checkerboard in perspective.

Lightly draw an "X" across the checkerboard, starting at each bottom front corner, cross in the center, and end up where the outside lines meet the horizontal line you drew earlier. Next, draw horizontal lines that cross where lines forming the "X" meet the lines that go to the vanishing point. There will be two crossing points everywhere except in the center of the "X." [Ref. 15, pp. 148, 149]

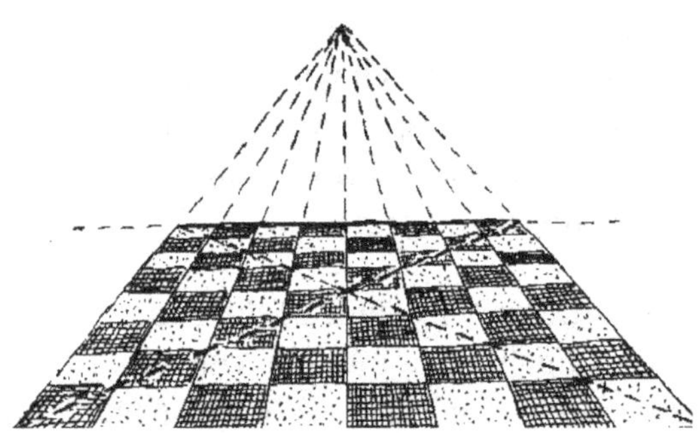

The Checkerboard

Use this technique to draw racks full of glasses or a room full of banquet tables. When you have found all the squares, draw one round shape in each square. Add vertical lines to give the glasses or tables height. Erase the "checkerboard" lines and finish the drawing.

Interior Perspective

Vincent Van Gogh's famous painting of his bedroom at St. Remy near Arles is cozy but looks a bit out of kilter. The two lower pictures on the right are askew. [Ref. 5, p. 67] I saw the actual room on a trip to the south of France a few years ago. It is on the second floor of the St. Remy asylum up a flight of cold stone steps from the ground floor. The wooden bed is gone, replaced with an iron one. A plaque on the wall tells visitors that the woman on whom the Dickensian character, Madam La Farge, of French Revolution notoriety was based was, at one time, confined there as well. There is a gift shop on the first floor where they sell paintings done by the residents. St. Remy is still used as a mental institution. On the way there we passed the bridge van Gogh painted in Arles. They have moved it from its original location to a small canal by the side of a paved two lane road. There is a sign and photograph of van Gogh's painting at the pull off area where the tour buses stop to give visitors a ten minute photo-op. The wooden bridge itself is now creosoted a black-brown color, unlike the fresh blond wood painted by van Gogh. The bridge was moved to its present location to make way for a more modern bridge. But the pictures on the bedroom wall make me wonder. Van Gogh knew about perspective. His painting of the "Terrace Cafe, Place du Forum, Arles, at Night" has it exactly right. [Ref. 5, p. 47] Maybe the pictures were hung crooked. Perhaps the painting, when reduced in size for a book, shows imperfections not obvious in the full sized painting. Maybe he made them that way on purpose!

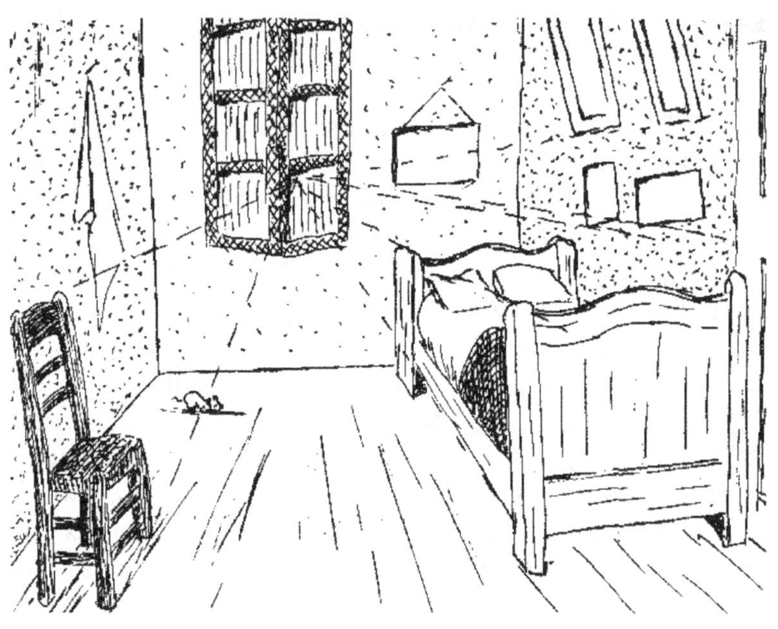

Interior Perspective

If you wanted to make a sketch of your own room, which happened to be similar to van Gogh's, how would you start? Using a ruler, follow the line formed by the long side of the bed to the window. Then draw a line to the window following the top of the chair on the left. The vanishing point is where the two lines meet. With the ruler at the vanishing point, find the line that would go underneath the two lowest pictures on the wall and straighten them up. Find the bottom of the left wall by taking a line from the vanishing point to the lower left corner of the back wall and extending it toward the foreground. Use the vanishing point you have found to help you place additional pieces of furniture in your room.

Drawing Round Vases and Tables

There is a painting by Henri Matisse (1869-1954) called "The Goldfish Bowl" which shows some goldfish in a glass of water on a table. [Ref. 7, p. 311] The back of the table seems to flip up at the viewer. Was this intentional or was it an accident? Was it characteristic of the slightly off beat way he painted? It is possible to draw table tops and vases so they don't look like they are flipping up.

Place a vase on a table and look at it closely. Notice how the mouth of the vase looks when you are standing, sitting in a chair, or sitting on the floor. Since most people view art at eye level, the mouth of the vase and the tabletop will look right when each is drawn as a narrow ellipse. Observe this easily in a transparent vase, an old fashioned oil lamp, or a water glass. The ellipse formed by the mouth may show up as only a line. If you are below it, it will be in the back and you will see it through the clear glass. As the vanishing point changes, the amount of visible table top and vase opening changes.

Most vases and tables are symmetrical. The simplest way to make both sides the same is to draw a vertical line to indicate the center of the vase or table. Measure in from the side of the paper to make sure the line is straight up and down. Draw one side of the table or vase the way you want it to look. Use a ruler and measure the distance from the center line to the side you have just drawn. Put a light pencil mark an equal distance on the other side of the line. Repeat this the length of the object. Connect the marks and both sides will look the same. If you have drawn it freehand, turn the paper upside down and check the symmetry, or add a center line and check it with a ruler.

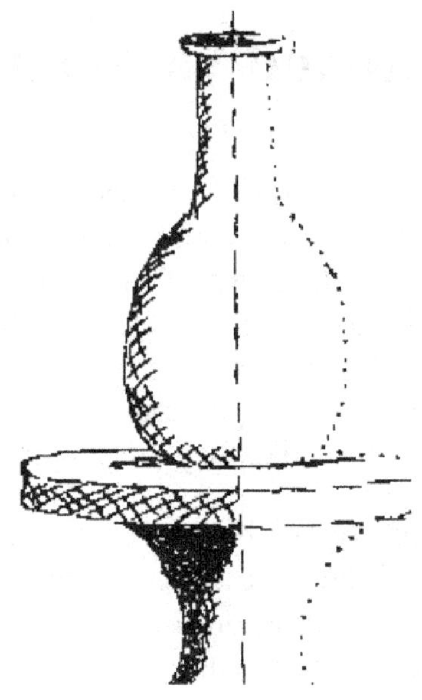

Drawing Round Vases and Tables

A light box can help you draw symmetrical objects. It has fluorescent bulbs inside and a translucent top. Place a drawing, with a center line lightly marked on it, on the light box with a piece of paper over it. Heavily trace the drawn side of the object and the center line. Flip it, place it underneath the original with the two center lines matched up and, following the tracing, sketch the missing side onto the original. Both sides will be identical. Make any object look grounded by drawing or painting a short horizontal line indicating shadow under it where it meets the table or floor.

Roof Peaks

We all know where to put the peak on an ordinary gable roof. It belongs at the top of the center of the side of a house, barn, or other building. We know exactly where to put it right up to the point where we have to do it, and then we eyeball it and say "I think that looks right, doesn't it?" Maybe it does and maybe it doesn't. I saw a painting of a house in an art show once where the roof peak was so wrong it was funny. If you don't know how to do it correctly, you will have trouble with it at some point. Learning this simple technique will save you from having any problem with roof peaks in the future.

Draw a house with two sides visible using basic perspective so that the far corners are slightly shorter than the middle one in the front. You know that the roof peak is directly above the center of the side of the building but, if you measure straight across the side and divide by two, the center will be in the wrong place. Vanishing point perspective moves the peak back. Draw an "X" on the side of the house from the base of the first floor to the base of the roof. Draw a vertical line up from the intersection of the two lines. The peak will be at a point of your choice on the vertical line. Roof heights vary, and as a result, not all roofs have the same slope. Draw lines from the peak to the corners of the building to form the roof.

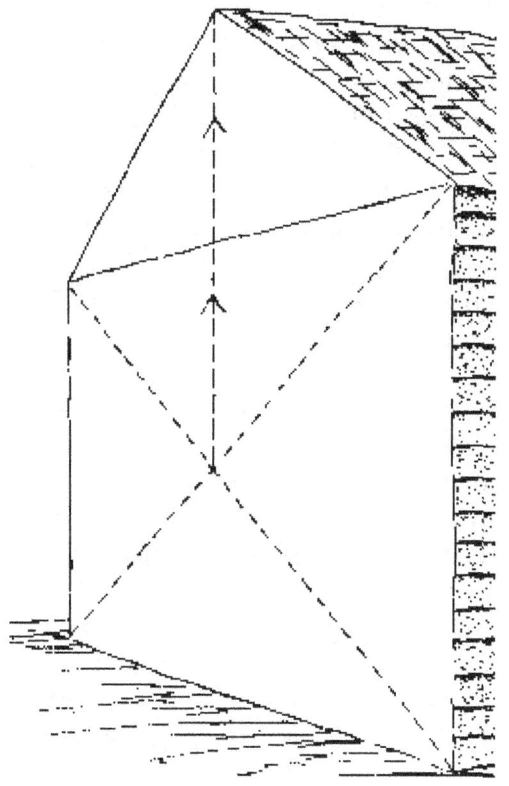

Finding the Roof Peak

Basic House

When I was seven years old my mother came into our half of the farmhouse we shared with my grandparents sputtering about how simple it was to draw a house. My grandmother was having trouble with it. Grandma Potter painted, but I didn't know much about her painting until years later. She painted on scraps of cardboard and linen book covers and had no supplies to share with her several grandchildren. Mother drew a simple house on our little blackboard and explained it to me. Since then I have seen the basic house drawn as a box with flaps. I have never forgotten how easy she made it look. The basic house uses vanishing points without actually showing them or making them seem difficult. In this drawing the vertical lines that form the end corners are shorter than the vertical line that forms the center corner in the front.

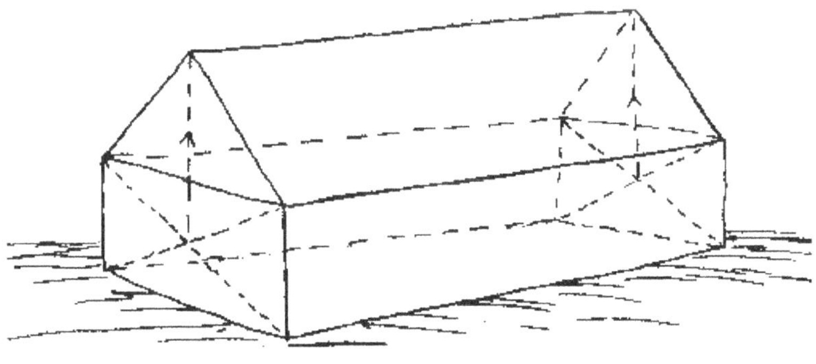

Basic house

If you were to show the lines to the vanishing points, they would lead to your visual horizon. In this case, the lines leading to the vanishing point on the left would be shorter than the ones leading to the right. If you aren't sure how to do this, look at your house from a distance, or look at a photo of it that shows two sides of a house. Follow the imaginary lines to the vanishing points made by the first and second floors as they lead away from it. The vanishing points are where the lines intersect.

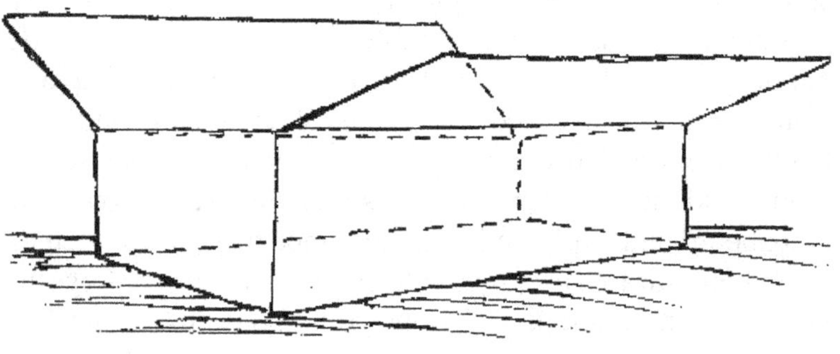

Basic box

Start the basic box or house by sketching vertical lines up from each corner with the front center one being a little longer than the other corner lines. The distance of the long side of the front should equal the long side in the back. Find the back corner and make its vertical line a little shorter than the other three corners. Connect all the vertical lines at the top and the bottom. When drawing the basic house, draw an "X" from the corners on the left side of the house as illustrated. Go straight up to find the peak. Draw another "X" on the inside of the house at the other end. Draw another line straight up. Place a roof peak on the first line at the height you prefer. Measure the length of the roof at the bottom where it meets the house. Place a top roof line of identical length from the first peak to meet the vertical line at the other end of the building. Move the roof line until it measures the same as the lower roof line while keeping it on the vertical line at the far end of the house.

Row Houses

If you have seen paintings by Maurice Utrillo (1883-1955), you know his street scenes are a delight of color and composition. [Ref. 7, pp. 291-293] How does one approach such a task? The difficulty seems to lie in determining the size of each building, and how they become smaller in the correct proportions as they disappear down the street. When you are figuring out how much to paint of a real street scene, you may find that there are more buildings than you want to include. Decide how many are necessary for the painting. The way to determine the size of each individual building is similar to the "X" technique used to determine the location of roof peaks. Think of the front area of all the combined buildings as one unit. Lightly draw an "X" over the entire area from the corners of the ground floor to the corners at the roofline. Draw a vertical line where the diagonal lines intersect. This produces one larger building and one smaller one. If you wish to subdivide these buildings, draw an "X" over the front of each one. Now there are four buildings, graduated in size to accommodate a sense of perspective.

Most paintings of row houses show one side of the street while showing only the near side of one house on the other side of the street. Drawing the same things on both sides of the street can sometimes look monotonous. But if there are row houses on both sides of the street, determine the sizes of individual units the same way and use a different vanishing point on the same horizon line for each side of the street. The only way the vanishing point would be the same for both sides of the street would be if the street ended at a vanishing point similar to that of a railroad track.

Once the buildings are in place, locate the doors and windows using the above technique. Center them the same way. Draw the "X" from corner to corner across the front of one row house. Find the mid point that indicates the center. Repeat this until the unit is divided up into small segments and you are able to place the doors and the windows.

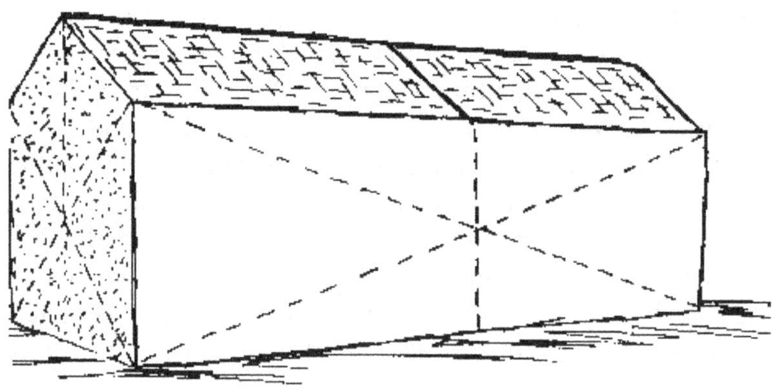

Finding the Size of Same Size Row Houses in Perspective

As an artist, you need to know if all the windows have the same type of construction. Do they all have window boxes for flowers? Do some have other design elements? Look at them closely. Are all the windows the same width and height? Are some directly above others? Do you want to include them all in the painting? Are some of them open? Do they have shutters? Have you used the vanishing point to line up the tops and bottoms of all the windows? I can see some of you deciding to avoid row houses, but once you understand the process it is not too difficult. With practice you will be able to estimate door and window locations fairly well.

Roofs on Row Houses

Roofs on row houses present new challenges. They sometimes have differing architectural elements that become complications for the artist. One row house may have a flat roof. Another may have a roof that slopes toward the street. Others may have peaks facing the street. Draw row houses like the basic box, two or three stories high. Find a roof peak on the side the same way as outlined previously. Then, pretend you can see through the row houses with x-ray vision, as shown in drawing the basis box type house, and find a roof peak farther down the street. Unless you are painting from a photograph, you may want to vary some of the details. Sometimes you will find that a flat roof on a row house has been transformed into a patio complete with flowers and trees in pots that are visible from the street.

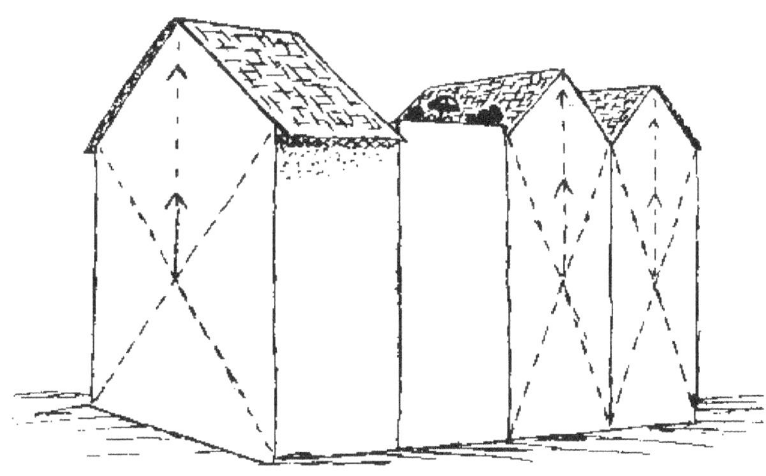

Roofs on Row Houses

If the row house roof has a peak facing the street, find it by using the front of the building. After you have determined its width, draw the "X" from the base of the roof to the ground floor. Draw a vertical line up from where the lines in the "X" cross. Place peak somewhere on that line. If there are several, do each one the same way. Keep in mind, that in this case, the ridge of each peaked roof facing the street will slope away from the street toward the vanishing point on the left. The height of each roof will vary as they follow a line to another vanishing point on the right.

Barn Roofs

Just when you thought it couldn't get any worse, eyeballing the placement of multiple ridges on a barn's gambrel roof is certain disaster. Once you understand it, however, the problem simply goes away. Farmers must have designed barns like this so they would have more room in their hay mows. My dad has a barn with a gambrel roof. On his barn two sheets of tin roofing material fit neatly from the top to the bottom edge of the roof, with a secondary roof ridge right where one sheet of tin overlaps the other. Some barns do not have equal sections. In those cases, you will need to change the location of the secondary ridges.

Here's how it works. Choose the vanishing points. Sketch the barn with two floors but without a roof. Lines leading to the vanishing point will indicate the ground floor and the top floor where it meets the roof. Draw the "X" across the side of the barn the same way you did to find the peak of the gable roof. Estimate where you want the peak to be. It should be about the height of one floor of the barn. Lightly pencil in the lines from the peak to the sides of the barn to form an ordinary gable roof with one peak. From the left side vanishing point draw a line to the peak that you have chosen. Draw another line from the same vanishing point so it falls halfway between the line leading to the peak and the line leading to the bottom of the roof. Continue these lines across the side of the barn to the other edge of the roof. Draw vertical lines straight up from both corners past the roof. Pencil in a third line halfway between the gable roof lines and the vertical lines. Changing the position of this third line will vary the location of the secondary roof ridges. The secondary roof ridges are located where the middle lines going up intersect the middle lines from the vanishing point.

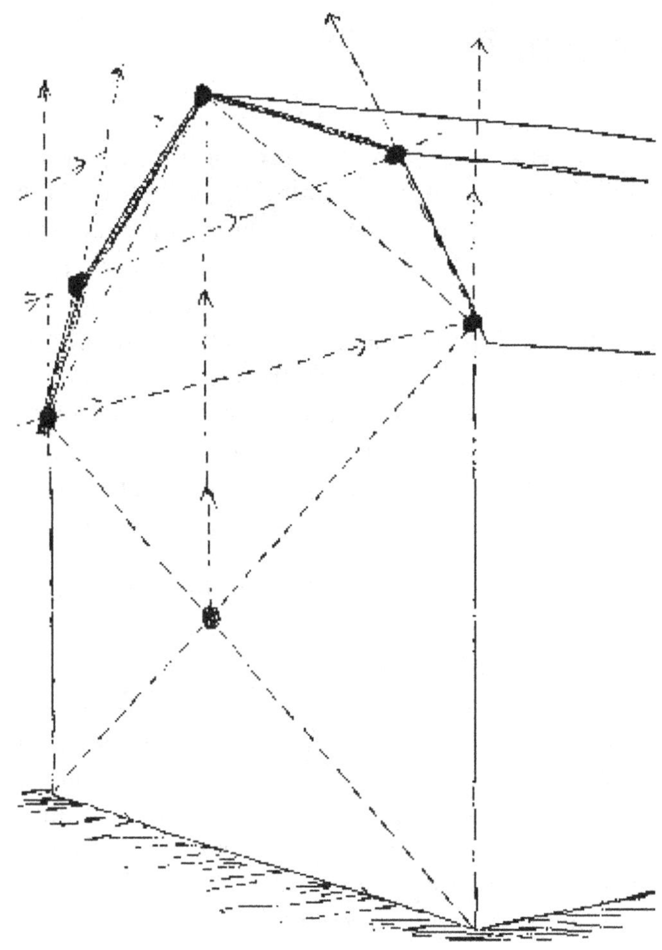

The Gambrel Barn Roof

The next problem to consider is where to put the far right end of the roof. The bottom of the roof line leads to the vanishing point on the right. Draw a line from the top peak to the vanishing point on the right. Measure it and make sure the roof ridge at the top is the same length as the bottom of the roof. Draw a line from the secondary roof ridge to the vanishing point on the right, making this part of the roof the same length as the top and bottom. Double check this, if you wish, by drawing the interior of the right side of the barn and finding the roof peak using the "X" across the side. The line straight up from where the lines forming the "X" intersect should connect with the end of the top ridge of the roof. This system can seem complicated at first, but it does work.

If there is a cupola on the top of the barn, treat it as a separate small building with the same problems as the barn, with one or more roof ridges using the same vanishing points as the barn. The entire roof of the cupola may not be visible due to the location of the viewer and the vanishing points.

Pennsylvania Bank Barn

If you have never seen a Pennsylvania bank barn with driveways on two levels, you may have seen a picture of one. Farmers didn't have elevators, but they still had to get things to different floors of the barn. Long ago someone decided to put a barn against the side of a small hill, a bank, and put a driveway and door on the first and second levels. Artists then had to figure out how to draw the whole thing. My painter grandmother had a very tough time with this one.

Begin by drawing the barn as a two story building with a roof without worrying about the upper level driveway. Once the two story barn is drawn, erase the line indicating the front of the basement floor. Bring the ground line along the side of the first floor of the barn, almost to the left corner. Let it slope down gradually toward the left. Show a few foundation stones. Take the ground down around the corner so it gradually falls away and exposes the lower entrance. Draw dirt driveways with wheel tracks to the doors on both levels.

The right side of the barn, also banked but unseen here, would typically have a high center haymow door, hinged at the bottom, that would open outward, with the help of a rope and pulley, and hang flat against the side of the barn. A farmer's helper would throw bales from a hay wagon to a motorized chain and paddle hay elevator which would convey the bales up to the haymow door where they would fall into the haymow. The farmer would stack them, gradually raising the level of hay until it reached the height of the door. In earlier times this was done with a system of boomerang shaped hay forks that locked in place until released, pulleys, horses and loose, unbaled hay. Today's huge round bales are not stored in hay mows because they are too big and difficult to manage. They are moved with fork lifts to sheds or covered in plastic and left at the edge of the field.

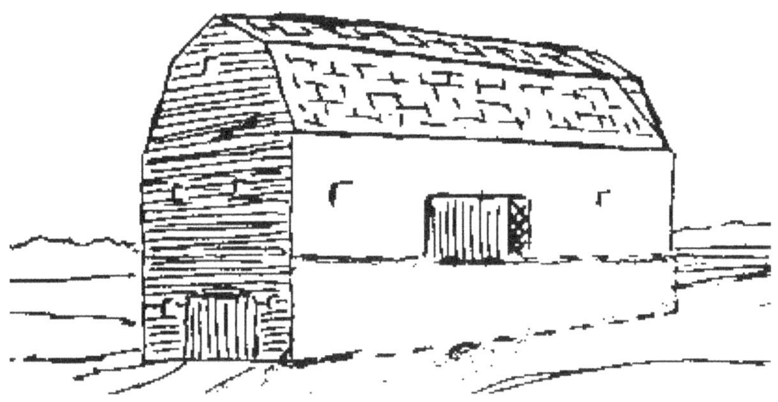

Draw the barn first as a building with only one ground level.

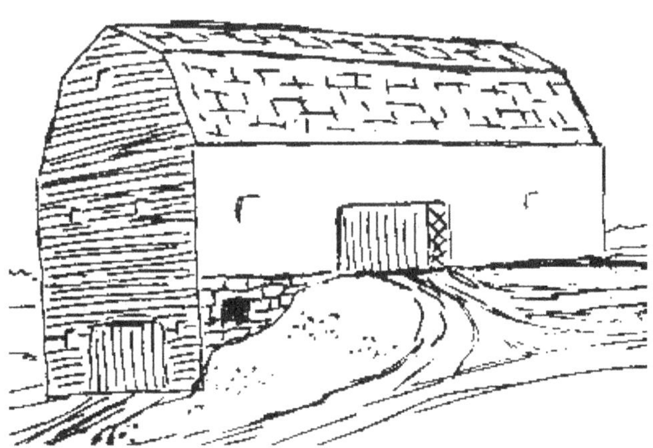

*Erase the basement line and add a driveway and
bank to meet the upper doorway.*

Buildings on a Hillside

I opened an art magazine and couldn't believe my eyes. An artist had painted a mountain scene containing buildings and the roof lines of all the buildings sloped downhill. The effect of this was that the buildings appeared to be slowly sliding down the mountain. The disaster was undoubtedly magnified by the fact that the pictures in the magazine were reduced in size compared to the originals. This often causes problems, unnoticed in full sized paintings, to become serious defects. If you are going to put something in a magazine or on a postcard, photocopy it first at a reduced size to make sure everything looks right when the image is made smaller.

When drawing buildings on a hillside, draw the sides of each building down to meet the mountain with the eaves of the roof and one side of the building forming something close to a ninety degree angle. As the drawing develops with the buildings roughly where you want them, find their vanishing points and double check to make sure that all the rooflines do not appear to be going downhill. Draw the first floor and a tiny bit of the foundation, perhaps made of stone, upon which the building rests. If you still have trouble with this, lightly sketch the whole building. When finished, sketch the mountain over it so that the building just peeks out from the side of it. Erase the parts that are behind the mountain. If it seems difficult, make the roof ridges horizontal until you figure out where the vanishing points are located. Adjust them as necessary. The buildings will all have the same two vanishing points. You may be able to avoid the problem encountered by the unfortunate artist whose buildings appeared to be sliding downhill.

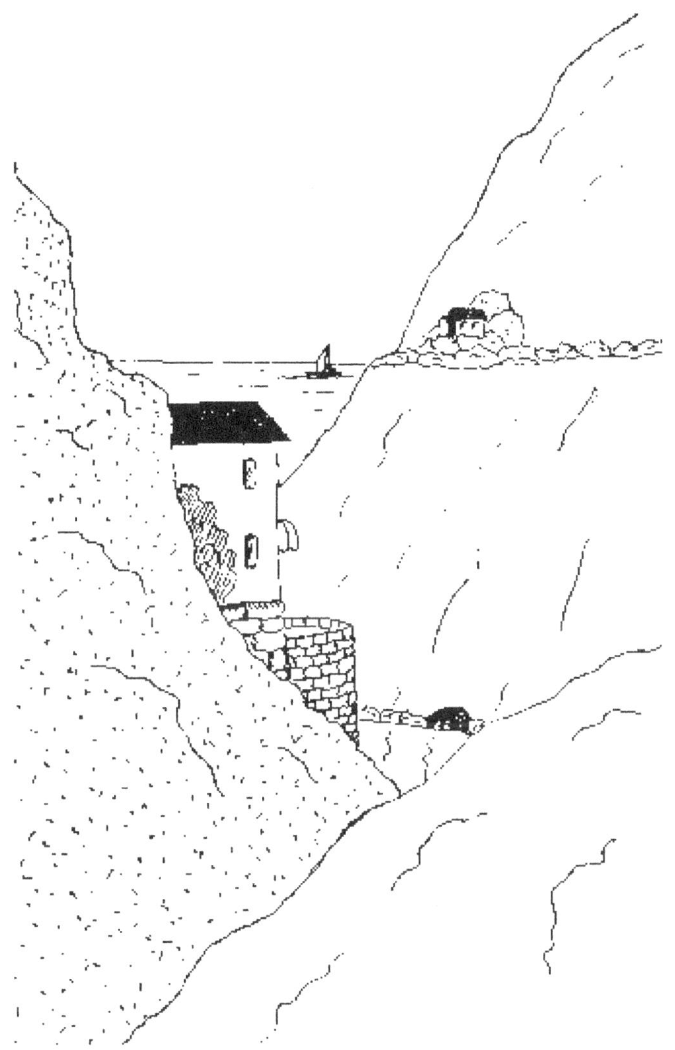

Buildings on Hillsides

Perspective from Above

Pittsburgh artist Doug Cooper skews and plays with perspective so that his city scenes are all topsy turvy. He works perspective every which way. He looks up and down streets and steep hills and chooses his vanishing points with skill and whimsy. Streets and houses swirl around telephone poles and cars in dizzying array. As crazy as it seems, it has a certain charm and Cooper is known for this type of drawing. He has played with perspective and made it do things for him. The vanishing points are where his eyes are looking at any given time and they are everywhere. He packs drawings of cityscapes together until they look simultaneously real and unreal. One of his murals is at the History Center in Pittsburgh. His drawings are fun. The buildings evoke a crazy quilt feeling but familiar Pittsburgh scenes and landmarks remain identifiable.

When you are upstairs looking into a basement, or in an airplane looking down, things fall into place visually in an order determined by perspective. As you are look straight down at a city intersection from above, the lines formed by the corners of the buildings lead to the vanishing point. With a little practice you'll understand how it works. As your skill improves you may also find it fun to play with perspective and make it do interesting things!

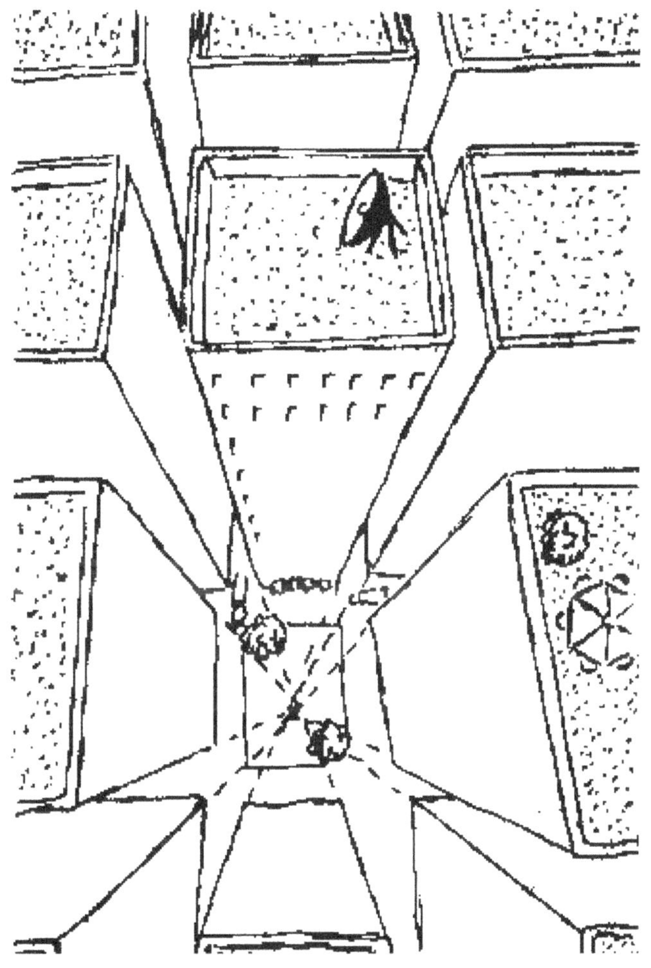

View from Above

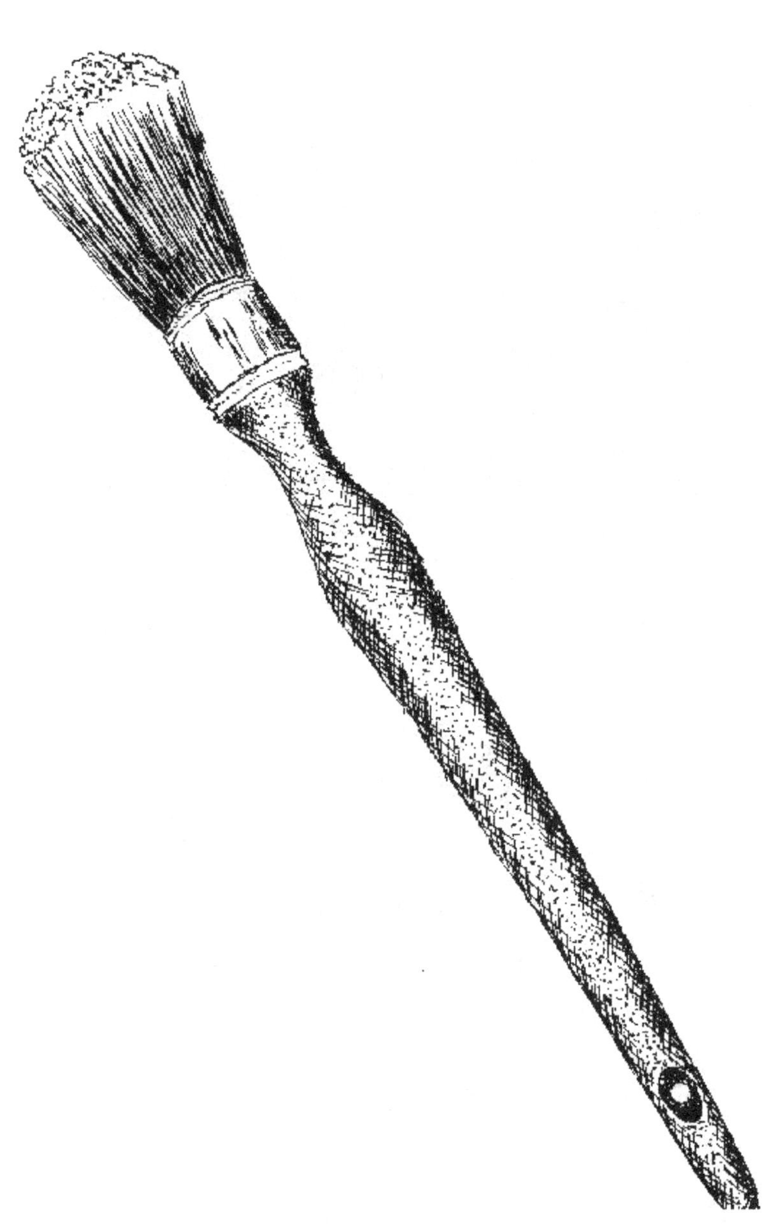

Oil Wash Brush

How to Paint Things

- **Portraits**
- **Painting Things that are "White"**
  - **Fog**
  - **Shadows**
  - **Clouds**
  - **Smoke**
  - **Snow**
- **Outdoor (Plein-Air) Painting**
  - **Water**
  - **Reflections**
  - **Windows**
  - **Left Sides**
  - **Trees**
  - **Flowers**
  - **Birds**
  - **Rocks**
  - **Beaches**
  - **Atmospheric Perspective**
- **Painting when you Travel**

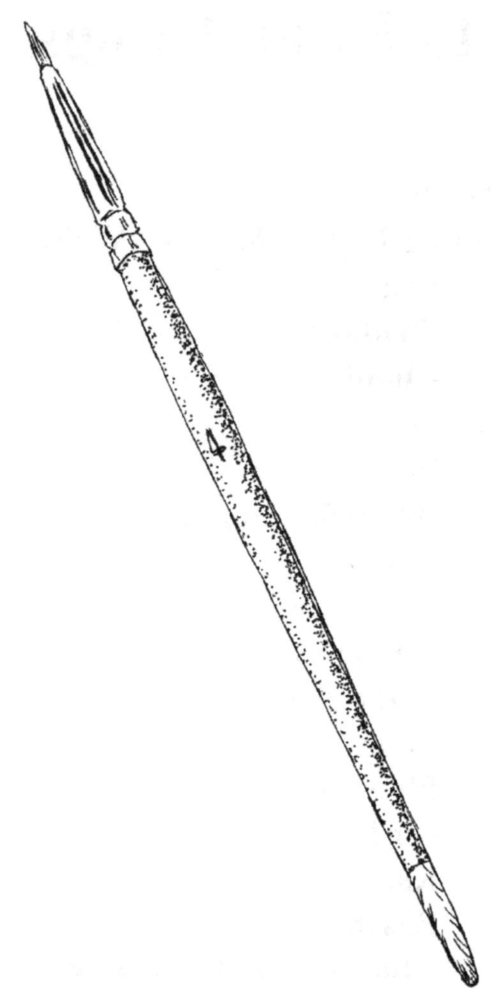

No. 4 Round Brush for Watercolor Painting

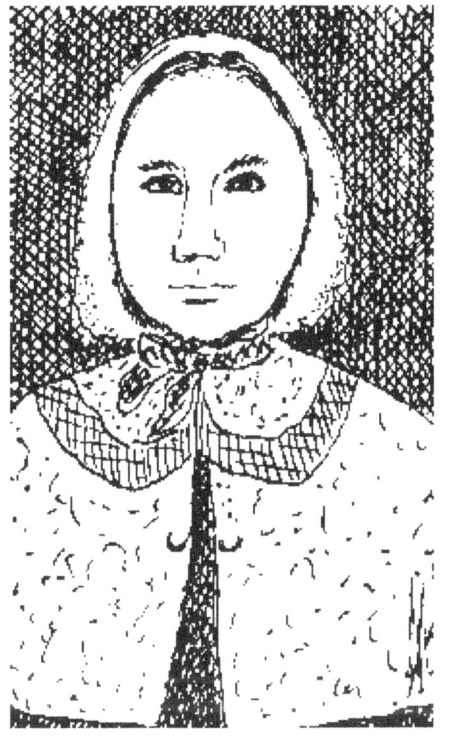

Portraits

An artist who can paint acceptable portraits can make a living doing it. In the long distant past portraits of important, wealthy people were a way of keeping an historical record. Portraits, usually painted taller than they are wide to fit the shape of the subject, of ordinary people became important with the Impressionists. Study portraits by famous painters and observe how the subjects are positioned, what colors the artists used, and what clothing or other details they included in the paintings.

We have all seen the traditional portrait of the patriarch or matriarch, dressed in finery, looking straight at the viewer. Gilbert Stuart's familiar, almost finished, portrait of George Washington is a good example. He looks very presidential. The founding fathers were often painted with very pale foreheads and rosy cheeks. They wore hats when they rode around their plantations but sunscreen hadn't been invented yet. Since everyone works at or is interested in something, try to include some clues about the person's interests in the portraits you paint. In James (Jamie) Wyeth's (1946-) "Portrait of Lincoln Kirstein." [Ref. 4, p. 167] The whole painting is in shades of black except for Mr. Kirstein's head, collar, and the buttons on his sleeve. The artist captures a stunning profile with an attitude and a glimpse of the man's personality. Mr. Kirstein looks like a decisive, intelligent, energetic person.

Andrew Wyeth (1917-) is also a master of capturing the spirit of his subjects in portraits. In "The Patriot" we see the pride in the old soldier's greenish-gray eyes, then realize he is wearing a German uniform from World War I. [Ref. 4, p. 146] A painting which could be considered a double portrait, "The Keurners" practically screams "dysfunctional family." [Ref. 4, p. 127] Mr. Keurner, followed by his wife, is walking off to the left about to go through a doorway where a brown door allows Mr. Keurner's face to show up nicely as light against dark. The painting is done in shades of dark brown and white. Mr. Keurner is wearing a warm looking dark brown coat with a furry collar. His wife, meek and downtrodden looking, has a white hat tied to her head, and wears a sheer print top with short sleeves over a brown sweater. A gun barrel at elbow height in the foreground, goes across the side of Mr. Keurner's body. The gun is aimed squarely at Mrs. Keurner. We cannot see if anyone is actually aiming the gun, or if it is resting on some unseen support. The effect is disturbing but it does tell us something about how the artist perceived them.

Portraits can be of animals as well as people. James Wyeth has done some wonderful animal portraits. A few years ago I saw him being interviewed on TV about his portrait of an enormous pig. [Ref. 4, p. 63] I saw the painting later at the Brandywine Museum in Chadd's Ford, Pennsylvania. It was the largest pig portrait I had ever seen. Go to any state fair and look at the largest pigs there and you will know how big it was. It was much bigger than "sofa sized." He measured and measured and fed the pig candy bars to keep it standing still, apparently for weeks, if not months, until he finished the painting. Good artists measure. They use rulers, thumbnail sketches, and anything else that works as a tool for getting the painting done well. I kept thinking about that pig painting. At first I wondered where one would hang such a painting. After a while I could imagine it hanging anywhere. It would look great in a dining room with a sense of humor or in any home with enough space around it to let it be a focal point. Wooden floors and colonial furniture would go well with it. I still can't get it out of my mind. I probably should have mortgaged the house and bought it. Well, maybe not, but outstanding portraits, human or otherwise, grab one's attention and they don't let go.

"Portrait of Lady" is another wonderful animal portrait by James Wyeth. A yellow sky comes one-third of the way down the painting, with dark land continuing to the bottom. [Ref. 4, p. 183] Lady is one very alert looking sheep. She has a black face and black ears that stick straight out horizontally. Her intense eyes look directly at the viewer. Her head and ears are framed by creamy white wool fleece, and she is positioned so that the length of her back is well above, and parallel to, the horizon. Her head is turned toward us. The fleece is fluffy, painted as somewhat matted clumps. One gets the feeling that James Wyeth managed to persuade Lady to stand still for a long time, too. "Portrait of Pig" and "Portrait of Lady," are stunning examples of animal portraiture. [Ref. 4, p. 63, 183]

Lesser known artists also paint animals. Pet owners love to own or paint portraits of dogs, cats, horses, or other animals. I entered an art show once where most of the prize winners turned out to be paintings of cats. I doubt if the judge even realized what she had done. Later I painted a portrait of a rooster named Chanticleer. My friends and I had gone to a farm to paint. As I tried to decide what to paint, the rooster crowed incessantly, so I painted him crowing. He was a great model and kept crowing while I worked. Chanticleer had charisma and his portrait turned out to be one of my favorites. Animals make good subjects and many artists like to paint them.

The Impressionists painted portraits of ordinary people. They were the first to do so. Van Gogh's portrait of Dr. Gachet conveys a feeling of "what's the use." [Ref. 5, p. 71] The weary looking doctor is leaning on his right hand with his elbow on a table. Some books and a potted plant are in the foreground. He is wearing a light colored cap and a dark overcoat with the top button open. He has a moustache. Tufts of reddish hair stick out between the bottom of his cap and his ears. Van Gogh's strokes of oil paint move the background and form the roundness of Dr. Gachet's sleeves and coat.

Gauguin painted portraits of Polynesian women in their native settings. Renoir painted French women in fine clothing. There are and have been many wonderful portrait painters and some who weren't so good. There are also those of us who draw until our doodles all look like Picasso's abstract portraits. The difference is that Picasso could draw and paint beautifully when he wanted to. The rest of us struggle to get it right and end up with the eyes misplaced all over the head quite easily. My sister's friend did a charcoal portrait of her. It looked like the top of her head was missing. Remember the old game where you change faces by substituting various blocks for the eyes, lips, chin, and so on? It reminded me of that game. Her artist friend didn't know that she should have placed the eyes close to the vertical center of the head, about halfway between the bottom of the chin and the top of the hair. My sister treasures the portrait anyway. To paint good portraits, one must study both good and bad examples. There is more to any portrait than just a face. Study the subject carefully, and try to capture its alertness, downtrodden attitude, sassiness, or spunk. Figure out where the personality traits show up. It could be the eyes, the turn of the mouth, the profile, or something else. Remember to get a firm idea in your mind of just how you want the whole thing to look when it's done, and resist the temptation to paint ornate, badly done, scenery in back of the subject. Keep the background simple and focus on the person or animal being painted.

When painting a human subject, as mentioned before, keep the eyes fairly near the vertical center of the head with about one eye's width between them. Avoid the natural tendency to make the eyes larger than they are. If doing watercolor, brush water over the face, except for the eyes, and drop in a skin colored wash containing a mixture of yellow, brown and red paint. Add a little extra pink color to the cheeks. For darker skin tones begin with orange and add dark blue with brown. Lift a highlight at the tip of the nose and on the forehead. Paint eyebrows and eyelashes one hair at a time with a tiny brush and angle them away from the center of the face. Put a little water on the corners of the eyes and drop in a tiny bit of Payne's gray to give the eyeballs roundness. Pick up excess water with a squeezed dry, splayed brush. Wet, then paint, the iris and the pupil except for the tiny spot you leave white as a reflection in exactly the same location on both eyes. If necessary, use white acrylic paint for the dot of reflected light. Add a thin gray line of shadow at the bottom of each eyeball. Remember the eyes have a little curve near the nose as well as a fold of skin above them. Don't draw the lips on with lines. Paint lips and soften the edges by going over them with a slightly dampened, larger brush. Lift off some of the color on the fullest part of the lower lip for a highlight with an almost dry wedge brush in watercolor or paint a soft edged highlight on it in oil. If your subject wears glasses, draw the glasses first. Indicate reflections on the lenses and metal frames. These can be just unpainted streaks or curves where the white of the watercolor paper shows through or white paint on canvas. Don't be afraid to paint some dark color in the nostrils and in the corners of the mouth. Remember to draw the tear duct in each eye near the nose. To paint the hair with watercolor, go over the hair area with a light wash. While it is still damp, drop in darker colors. After it dries, streak on some darker individual hairs. In oil, paint lighter, single hairs on last. Soften them with an almost dry brush if necessary. It helps if you have a model or a good photograph. If the subject is backlit, with the front in shadow, show the color of the light on the edges of hair, face, and clothing. Give it a soft edge as it blends into the shadow.

Some portraits include hands. Others don't. Did you ever wonder why some portraits show a person with his hands in his pockets? Even John Singer Sargent did that at least once, in a wonderful, full length portrait of a man. If you have trouble painting hands, a pocket is a really good place to put them. But, if you do want to draw a hand, draw the shape of it first, like a mitten. Then put in the thumb and fingers. Note where the bone is on the wrist. I saw a painting in a magazine on which the artist had painted an extra finger by mistake. She noticed it later and it was mentioned in the accompanying article. One can get mixed up painting hands. Keep in mind whether you are painting the left or the right hand and you will be able to figure out where the thumb should be.

A portrait will sometimes show an arm or a leg in a foreshortened pose. Foreshortening is difficult for some artists because they know the arm or leg is long, but it is bent in such a way that it doesn't take up much space. Measure body parts or clothing against each other to place foreshortened parts. Practice this without drawing. Get in the habit of "drawing" with your eyes wherever you find yourself. Notice where things are in relation to other things when you look at them. One person's head may reach the shoulder of another. Keep measuring the parts of objects as they relate to other parts and don't limit it to portraits. If you can do this effectively, foreshortening will not be a problem in your paintings.

Study portraits done by great artists. Borrow ideas from them and add some creativity of your own. A portrait, though usually a front view, can be a back view or profile if it portrays the essence of the subject's personality. Study your subject carefully and produce a good drawing by measuring all the features against adjacent ones. Add indications of the subject's personality or occupation and you will be well on your way to painting good portraits.

Painting Things that are White

If you've ever chosen the white paint for a room, you know there are many shades of "white." Painting things white, therefore, is not as simple as letting the color of the paper show through. Sometimes when you paint things you know to be white, like flowers, snow, and clouds, you may be tempted to actually make them plain white but even "white" snow is often not really white. Whites always look better when you add bits of delicate light colors to them.

I noticed a watercolor portrait of a doctor in a white jacket on the wall of a hospital waiting room. I found it interesting because the jacket, instead of being pure white, had very light touches of yellow and pink in the un-shadowed areas and similar brush strokes of blue, lilac and gray in the shadows. In some places the colors were painted over each other. The colors were mixed delicately, and yet, the jacket was white. Adjacent dark colors make light colors look whiter and brighter. The background of the doctor's portrait contained gray just dark enough to make the jacket look white even though it contained many pastel shades. Part of the fun of painting is in mixing up the colors so the paint itself becomes interesting. Keep working until you achieve the result you want.

Fog

Objects barely visible in fog have soft, indistinct edges. A yellow sun about to burn off the early morning fog and two people walking toward it will all have soft edges and muted colors. The backs of the people will be softly shadowed. In watercolor wet the paper with a clear water wash. Let it flash off and then indicate what you are seeing through the fog by dropping in small amounts of yellow for the sun and Payne's gray and hints of skin and clothing color for the people. Don't put in much detail. Drop in just a little color and keep the shadowed figures mostly in gray tones. Indicate trees and buildings the same way. Paint depth and variations in the fog by dropping in some very pale lilac or gray and pale yellow in other places to give the fog a feeling of volume. Think of it as the inside of a cloud. If the paper starts to dry, add a little more water. Don't let the edges dry hard. Keep them soft and fuzzy. Let the fog, meaning the water on the white of the paper, bleed into and over the figures and the sun without leaving any hard edges.

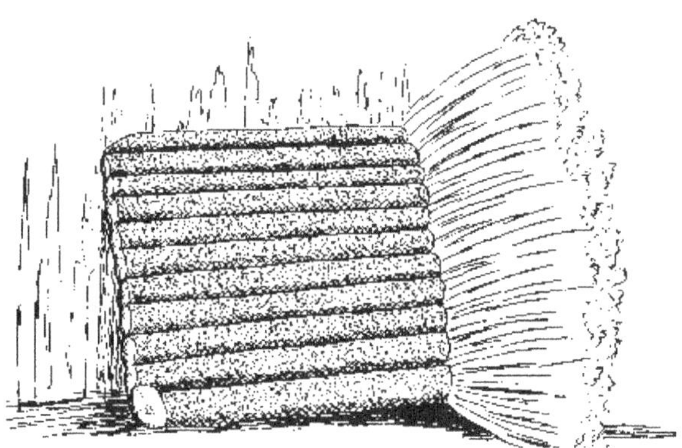

Chinese watercolor wash brush: nice, but sheds like a cat.

Shadows

Shadows fall from one or more light sources when an object interrupts a stream, or streams, of light. Adding a line of shadow at the bottom of it will make it appear to be anchored to a base. A bumpy subject will have bumpy shadows. For example, tire tracks in the snow will have shadows that go up and down over the high and low spots. When working in watercolor, paint all the detail first without any shadow, then add a glaze of Payne's gray mixed with the complement of the underlying color. The detail should show through the shadow as it would in real life.

Can shadows do something in addition to interrupting a stream of light? Definitely! A shadow on the wall of a person in a distinctive shape, such as a military uniform, can tell the viewer who else is there without putting that person in the painting. Similarly a shadow of a tree or a building can indicate their presence outside the boundaries of the artwork. In Charles M. Russell's oil, "When Shadows Hint Death," [Ref. 2, p. 60], two cowboys are leading their horses single file up a steep hillside on the right toward the viewer. Each man has one hand tightly gripping his horse's nose just above the nostrils to prevent it from making any noise. On a yellow ochre mountain across the valley to the left, the men have noticed the shadow of an Indian war party on horseback at the top of the shadow of the mountain they are climbing. It makes them aware of the danger on the ridge just above them. The shadows are muted lavender-gray and do not attract attention at first. The cowboys and horses make a nice picture, but the shadow of the war party adds a whole new dimension to the work and is the essence of the painting.

Clouds

A new painter's first inclination may be to paint a blue sky with big fluffy white cumulus clouds. Maybe we just don't go out to paint when it is raining, snowing, or when the sun is obscured by a low, heavy blanket of gray stratus clouds. Blue skies are great, but don't forget about the other ones. The dark sky with violent black nimbus clouds, yellow light and strong shadows right after a storm can be very dramatic, too. Changes in weather and time of day produce interesting clouds and skies.

A seascape once hung in the Victorian style lobby of a boardwalk hotel in Ocean City, Maryland. From a distance it looked alright, but close inspection showed that the clouds were painted just like waves in the ocean. They could have been lowered right into the water and they would have been perfect! Clouds and waves are not the same. If you spend some time looking at clouds you will be able to tell cirrus from cumulus. Nearby clouds usually look bigger while the distant ones appear smaller. Often the cloud bottoms will be in shadow. In this case, the artist knew the sea, but had not paid much attention to the sky above it.

Form clouds in watercolor by lifting color from a wet sky. Squeeze a large round brush almost dry. Splay the bristles and push it against the wet paint. Rinse and repeat. Another way is to leave some of the wet paper white when doing the sky wash. Either way, add some delicate colors to the wet, white clouds to give them shape and volume. Don't hesitate to experiment. Let skies show the mood you want to convey but do a little cloud gazing before you paint them.

Smoke

Smoke has a billowy, translucent quality and sometimes has flames around and through it. Smoke can, but doesn't always, indicate terrible disaster. The day and night steel mill paintings by Aaron Harry Gorson (1872-1933) show heavy industry at work. [Ref. 2, pp. 51, 54, 55] His oil paintings of Pittsburgh are interesting today because most of the mills are gone. The smoky night scenes show the mills and lights around them reflected in the river. Today, when Pittsburghers see his paintings, they often comment about how much gritty dust was on their window sills every day when the steel mills were in operation. In the 1950's, there was so much smoke in Pittsburgh that by noon men's white shirt collars were filthy with coal dust and ladies' slips were streaked black with it. Street lights were on during the day because it was so dark. That era is gone now and Pittsburgh is a clean, beautiful city with all the amusements three rivers can provide. Gorson's paintings serve as an historical record of a time when American steel was king. In his day he painted what interested him, not knowing it would be gone in the future.

To paint smoke in watercolor, begin by brushing water over the area to be filled with it. When it flashes off, drop in orange, yellow, and red to indicate flame, or blue for sky where appropriate. Leave gaps in the color. After it dries, re-wet it and drop gray, brown, black or purple smoke in the gaps. Vary the intensity of the colors to produce a feeling of depth and volume.

Snow

There are two types of snow to consider for our purposes: snow on the ground and snow falling in the air. The easiest way to paint fallen snow is by looking through a window from a nice warm room. The worst way is to be outside in freezing weather. A compromise of sorts can be found by painting outside on a deck at a ski resort lodge. A warmly dressed artist can sit, paint, and go back inside for a hot chocolate when the weather gets too cold. Sometimes, when it's above freezing, there will be a fine mist in the air. This works amazingly well on watercolor paper, providing just enough water to make the paint move beautifully, without the need for a clear water wash first, as the colors and the mist work together

Snow on the ground in a watercolor painting begins as the white of the paper. The artist adds color in the form of shadows as well as reflections of sky colors or man made light such as neon signs or brake lights. Watercolors of sunny snow scenes look brighter if you brush the top of an open snow covered space with some clear water, let the shine flash off and drop in some very pale yellow to indicate sunshine. Use watered down Prussian blue, Payne's gray, or purple to depict shadows. When drawing and painting snow, notice the way it wraps around trees and buildings, sometimes leaving a nicely rounded snow free area. Observe its shadows, the way it drifts and blows, how it covers some things and leaves others bare. Try to capture the quiet of the storm's aftermath.

Falling snow is painted last in both watercolor and oil. Generally, if you want to paint something white in watercolor, the actual white should be the white of the paper showing through but in this case it is acceptable to use diluted artists' acrylic paint in tubes or liquid acrylic paint sold in fabric stores. Pour a small amount of either paint on a palette. Dip the bristles of a toothbrush in the liquid paint. With the loaded toothbrush bristles up, and the painting on a flat surface, pull your thumb or forefinger quickly toward your body as you stand in front of, but not directly above the painting. Practice this before doing it over an important work because it can drip and get messy until you understand how to do it. If you are painting an interior scene with a snowstorm going on outside the window, mask part of the painting by covering it with paper cut to expose only the part that will have snowflakes. Remember to mask window dividers. Don't worry if small imperfections appear in the spray from the toothbrush. They will make the result look more like a snowstorm. Whether you paint snow on the ground or falling snow, try to capture the moment. If the wind is blowing, the snow will be swirling or blowing in a certain direction with other things in the painting bending or blowing away.

My grandmother, Lois Sterling Potter (1895-1968), circa 1940, painted an oil of my grandfather behind a "V" shaped, flat bottomed snow plow being pulled by a team of work horses, a strawberry roan on his left and a white horse named Silver on his right. They face left in blue shadowed snow with Silver's nose ahead of the roan's. Evergreen trees on a hill at the far right are separated from them by an unseen road below a snow bank. Grandpa kept the horses as pets after World War II when it appeared that they had been replaced permanently by tractors. How strange it is to see a snow plow being pulled by horses when plows are generally pushed by vehicles today!

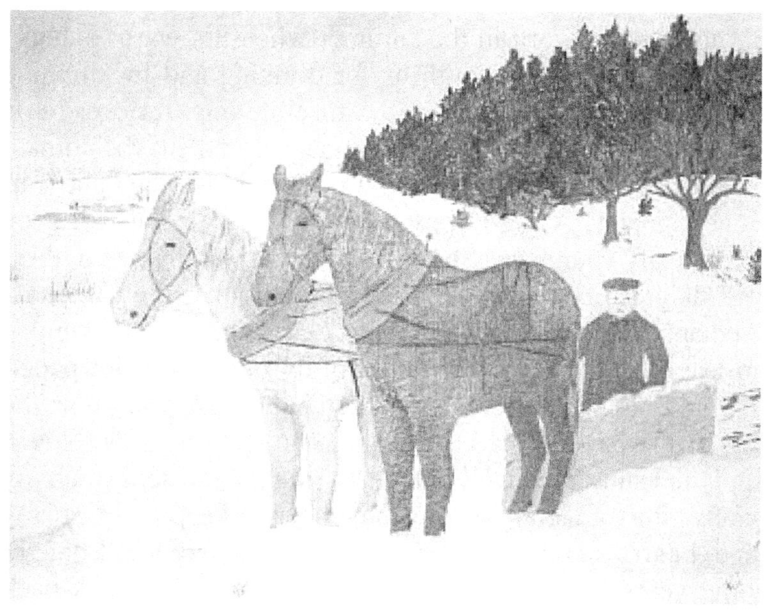

"Pa and His Horses"
Oil painting by Lois Potter, the author's grandmother

Outdoor (Plein Air) Painting

"En plein air" (pronounced 'on plan air') is French and means "outdoors." In the past it referred to an Impressionist group and their use of light and shadow. Claude Monet (1840-1926) painted on his boat, in his garden, and at the beach. He painted beauty in the sea, in his flower garden, in haystacks, and cathedrals. He found everyday scenes and translated them into masterpieces with his paints. He painted real things. In his day the haystacks were ordinary, but in our time, besides being beautiful paintings, they show another way of farming. As a plein air artist today you preserve history when you paint the simple things of daily life outdoors.

Some plein air artists paint outdoors all year round, but most of us work in the summer when it's warm outside. We always take water with us for drinking and for thinning watercolors, acrylics, and water miscible oils. It never hurts to pack a few snacks, raisins, bananas, and maybe tomato juice or soft drinks. Forget about potato chips. They get your fingers greasy. A big floppy hat with a wide brim will keep the sun off your face. Some artists wear sunglasses. Others feel they are better able to see true colors without them. I tried applying sunscreen just before painting once and ended up leaving a big greasy thumbprint on my watercolor paper. It would not come off and absorbed paint differently than the rest of the paper. I had to fix that one with scissors. Now I apply the sunscreen well before leaving the house. I wash my hands afterwards, and try to remember to keep them off my face. I carry supplies in a large canvas tote bag that I bought some years ago in Maine. Some artists carry a back-pack containing, among other things, a canvas and aluminum stool. I keep a beach chair, and a clamp-on umbrella for shade, in the trunk of my car. The beach chair is half the height of a lawn chair. It's close to the ground where I put my brushes and water, but it can be difficult to get out of when one has been sitting in it for a long time. In addition, I generally paint with distilled water just in case the minerals and impurities in tap water might cause discoloration or disintegration of the paper in the future. Not everyone worries about these things.

My friends and I often paint en plein air together during the summer. We feel safer in a group. We have painted in many locations where we would not have ventured alone. Painting outdoors can be a bit intimidating. Once you get used to it you will remember to take the insect repellent. There are other distractions. In resort areas, people may gather around and watch every brush stroke. This is unnerving at first, but as you experience it more often, you will gain confidence and learn to focus on the work. Even then it can still be disconcerting. Just continue painting or answer questions if they have any. People are curious by nature and it is flattering that they are interested in what your are doing. You might even sell them a painting!

Everything outdoors competes for the artist's eye. Some painters hold up a small mat, or two diagonally opposite corners of a mat, to form a frame around the scene they want to paint. Once you decide what you would like to paint, it is tempting to start painting right away, but it's better to draw the scene first and then paint.

Suppose you are doing a difficult sketch under a bridge or next to a boat dock attached to some steep steps. You may not have time to do a lot of thinking about thumbnail sketches and vanishing point perspective. There is an easy way to accurately sketch a landscape by first drawing on plexiglass as you look through it at the scene. If the first sketch doesn't work out, rub it off with a rag and start over. When you have finished, hold the glass a foot or two above the paper or canvas and, with you hand and pencil underneath it, copy the drawing.

Start with a small (approximately 8" x 10") piece of plexiglass and a grease pencil in a color other than black. The grease pencil is sometimes called a china marker and is available in craft stores. Buy the plexiglass at an auto glass place. Ask them to smooth the edges for you. If it is not the same proportion as the painting surface, see the section on transposing photos when the photo is too large. Instead of cutting the plexiglass, mark the picture boundary line on it with the grease pencil and stop the sketch at that line.

I saw this technique demonstrated at an art club meeting. I tried it a few weeks later. It is a little tricky at first. Hold up the plexiglass, look through it at the scene and draw it with the grease pencil. Don't worry about details. Trace only the main elements such as the horizon, building lines, big trees, height of figures, bridges and so on. The main difficulty is in holding the glass steady while you sketch. Each time you touch the grease pencil to it, refer to the first mark you made and make all the lines you have drawn fall on their counterparts in nature. The idea is to get just the basic structure of the picture on the plexiglass.

Hold the glass about 18 or 20 inches above the painting surface until the drawing covers it. Using a pencil, or charcoal for canvas, reach underneath the glass and copy the lines. Make sure you continue to hold the plexiglass the same distance from the paper as you copy the drawing onto the painting surface. Refer continuously to the starting point and make sure marks on the plexiglass match the real scene in nature and that the marks on the paper or canvas match the grease pencil lines. Any time you move the plexiglass, recheck all the pencil marks. If it doesn't look right, keep rechecking until the lines you have drawn on the glass match the scene and lines on the paper or canvas match the lines on the glass. If the grease pencil is a color other than gray or black, it is easier to see what you are copying. This method will get the basic elements, including perspective, down correctly. You won't have to worry about vanishing points. Continue to work on it outdoors or take it back to the studio with you.

This method may seem tricky at first but, with a little practice, you will find yourself able to get a difficult drawing done faster and more accurately than if you were to try to do it freehand.

Water

Sometimes new artists find it difficult to draw bodies of water without having the water look like it is standing up instead of being a nice flat surface. It may help to put a turn at the top of the stream to indicate that the source of the water is around a bend. It might also help to avoid vertical lines as shore lines and to remember that water, except for waterfalls and rapids, is always horizontal.

A stream, lake or ocean should not look like it is flipping up. The water may splash, but it always comes back to earth. The shore line may zig and zag, but it does not stand straight up, although it may have a few big rocks or small waterfalls that do. Once the drawing of horizontal water is on paper, it is easy to add waves crashing against rocks. Wave patterns in the foreground exist within the confines of a body of water that is horizontal in the distance as do the wide brush strokes indicating waves and reflections in the foreground of Monet's "La Grenouillere." You may find water difficult to paint but don't get discouraged. Every artist improves as time goes on. Even famous artists often have trouble painting water. Early Currier prints show waves in water as wide "u" shaped curved lines. As time passed he learned how to make better ones. Later Currier and Ives prints have much more natural looking waves. [Ref. 12, plate 166] Even though Currier had trouble getting the waves right, the bodies of water he drew were horizontal and did not flip up at the viewer.

The color of water is often not as blue as one might paint it. A few years ago I saw an amateur artist's campy oil painting of a Parisian living room with an ornate settee in

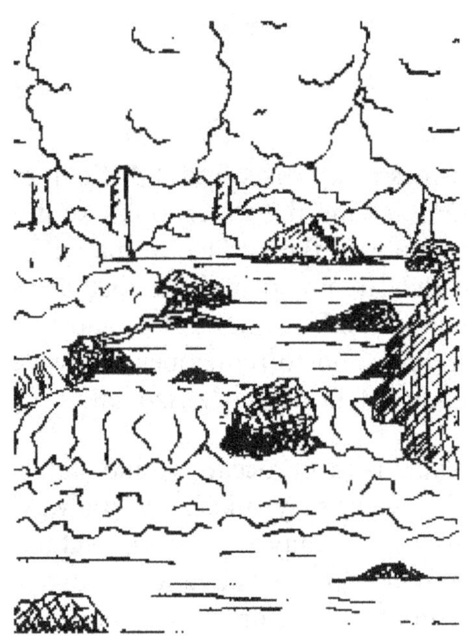

Water is horizontal except when it isn't.

front of an open window with the Eiffel Tower in the distance. The River Seine ran through the city. The sky was gray. The pure, right out of the tube, solid powder blue color of the river threw the whole painting off. Water often takes on the color of the sky, and like the sky, is rarely one flat shade of blue. Striations of various blues and other colors might have helped. As it was painted, however, the color looked noticeably odd. Take a really hard look at the color of water outdoors. Water takes its color from many things including the sky, trees, mud, rocks and algae. Add depth by adding dark green to the bluish water in the foreground of your painting.

To paint a waterfall in watercolor wet the area with clear water and drop in a few very pale vertical streaks of blue and greenish-gray paint as well as some light brown near the sides to indicate earth or rocks. Hold the paper up so the color runs down. The top of the waterfall should be somewhat uneven. Leave a lot of white with soft hints of color in it. Drop in some greenish-gray at the bottom and touch it with a dampened brush to soak up excess water and prevent hard edges from forming.

Ponds, oceans, lakes and rivers often reflect light as horizontal streaks. If you are using oil paints, add light colored streaks of paint to indicate reflections in the water. In watercolor, pull a brush loaded with clean water quickly across rough paper. It will leave dry spots. If the dry spots are too big or round, streak water and paint through them so they become streaks or small flecks of reflected light. Drop color into the wet areas and leave most of the dry spots white. Lift additional streaks while the paint is wet to show more reflections. Lift off lines of color with a half inch wedge brush. Dip it in water, wipe it off, squeeze it almost dry, and pull it across the still damp watercolor paint in slightly squiggly, horizontal lines. Do it randomly so it looks like reflected light, not stripes, in the distance. In the foreground, add some choppy waves or surf. The Impressionists were masters of this. Monet painted Etretat with its dappled water. Perhaps you will paint seascapes, as did Monet, from your own boat. Even if you can't, notice how a scene looks from various locations. A painting of a beach painted from the sea is quite different from one painted from the shore even though the water will be horizontal from both vantage points.

Reflections

Artists understand two kinds of reflections: images and light. Squint your eyes when you look for reflections of light and you will see the strongest ones. Water, metal, mirrors, and other shiny surfaces reflect both images and light. Reflections in water are always directly below the item being reflected. They are not, however, just an inverted version of reality. Turn the painting upside down to see if you are getting the shapes right. The edges of reflections will be a bit fuzzier than the real scene. There may be streaks of light in the water that will that cut through the images. The brightness of the colors may vary from the actual ones. Objects may not be reflected in their entirety due to the location of your vantage point.

In James Wyeth's painting "Portrait of Jeffery" white paint is squiggled over the lenses of Jeffery's eye glasses as reflected light. [Ref. 4, p. 165] There is even a straight white line indicating a crack on the right one. The metal frames of his glasses and the buttons of his coat reflect light. His glasses sparkle in an otherwise dark painting of a handsome young man's head and upper torso. He wears a dark, double breasted overcoat in front of a dark background. His skin tones are ruddy and he is not clean shaven, but he does not have a beard. The reflections enliven the painting.

Monet painted well known landscapes with reflections of poplars and water lilies. [Ref. 10, p. 138] In his painting, "Four Poplars," the trees form a line along the horizon and the foreground is full of their reflections. [Ref. 10, p. 135] The trees divide the canvas in equal segments and produce a strong geometric appearance. The predominantly aqua sky contains flecks of blue, pink, and yellow. Yellow

trees recede into the background on the left. The underbrush
along the edge of the water has some yellow topping it off on
the right, but it is generally the same color as the trees with
brown, rust, blue, and violet tones. The trees are skinny and
not exactly straight. Their reflections are cut off so that the
treetops are not visible. The color of the water is similar to
that of the sky. The painting shows geometric artistry as well
as painterly skill. Similar colors over the entire painting have
a unifying effect.

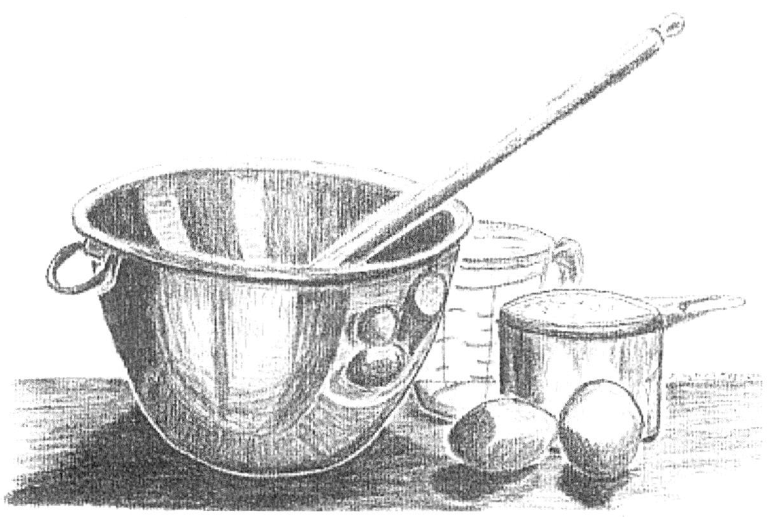

Charcoal Drawing: Reflections in a Bowl

Reflections in windows and in metal are more
complicated. A shiny bowl will have curvy reflections on its
side from nearby items. If you draw images as they are
reflected, it will look right. Reflections in metal and in water
require that you paint what you see on the reflective surface.
The metal surface may curve, distorting the objects it reflects
and the water surface may ripple and move. Glass can be
more complicated because, while there are reflected items to

paint, there may be a view through the glass that is visible in places where the reflection doesn't block it. A shop window reflecting a street scene may have merchandise in the window that competes with the reflections.

When painting ordinary windows with panes of glass reflecting blue sky, paint them one at a time. Let adjacent panes dry before you watercolor the ones next to them. When the shine flashes off paint pale Prussian blue sky color in the lower right corner and paint a gray shadow in the upper left corner of each pane. Lift out wavy streaks of both colors with a wedge brush before the paint dries to show reflected light. If you are doing a large window with many panes of glass, this will convey a feeling that each pane is reflecting the sky in a slightly different way. Glass covered "big box" buildings often reflect sunlight, clouds, and nearby buildings in glittering, spectacular fashion. Paint the large scenic reflections with a watercolor wash. Lift reflections of light while the paint is wet. Add inverted "L" accents at the top left corner of the window panes after the wash has dried. If the building is the focal point of the painting, paint each pane one at a time. If the building is one of several in a cityscape, paint each building with a wash and add details as necessary.

Windows

There is more to windows than just reflections. An open door or window can be a painting within a painting. The view may tell us more about the location. Andrew Wyeth used this technique in many paintings, including "Whale" where sun bleached whale bones sit on a dark shelf in a dark building with an open door and a view of the sea, where the whale once lived, in the distance. [Ref. 4, p. 149] The painting is much more interesting with the open door than it would have been without it.

Indicate small outside windows by drawing an inverted "L" in the top, left corner of each one to define it. Sometimes that's all you need. If the building is close enough to see all the window detail, draw the whole window and paint it. While painting it, darken the upper left corner as an inverted "L" to give it shape and depth. Add shadow, and lift some of it, to show reflected light. Please refer back to the section on reflections for more on windows.

Windows may have picturesque shutters. Vary details to make each window interesting. Show someone looking out the window, leaning out to talk to a neighbor, hanging laundry, or watering a flower box. Some shutters are large enough to cover the window when closed. Some can be propped open at the bottom. Some are left slightly ajar while still hooked together in the center. Notice where the windows are, how the shutters are attached, and make sure everything lines up correctly before you begin to paint.

Left Sides

When artwork looks flat, the artist has neglected to give volume to items in the painting. Using more intense color, as well as shadow, to shade and darken the left side of objects will give them definition and volume. This is especially noticeable in murals where painted scrollwork is used to form borders. Painted scrollwork looks like raised molding when the left side is shaded sufficiently. The illusion, sometimes called "trompe-l'oeil" (pronounced tromp-loy, French for "illusion"), produces, in this case, an illusion of real molding. This technique can be applied, sometimes humorously, to canvases or walls where the artist wants the viewer to mistake the painting for the real thing. A painting, directly on a wall, of an open door and a stairway in back of it that looks like a real door and real stairs is another example of trompe-l'oeil painting. The painted molding would have a hard edge on the left side and a soft edge on the right side. As the molding curves, the shadow jumps so it is still on the left side.

In addition to creating illusions, shading the left side of each item in a painting will give the work a harmonious appearance. This left side treatment works well on tree branches, flower blossoms, leaves and stems, windows and just about everything else. Bring gray and the complement of the object's color around the left side. Brush and blend the color toward the body of the object. Accentuating left sides of painting subjects will produce a consistent, unified work. It is a finishing touch that will make your paintings look better.

Trees

N.C. Wyeth's (1882-1945) painting "And Lawless, keeping half a step in front of his companion..." shows a huge gnarled, snow-covered tree in the background. [Ref. 4, p. 104] His "Robin Hood and His Companions Lend Aid..." shows the merry band shooting arrows in the shelter of a huge tree trunk with massive roots. [Ref. 4, p. 110] Wild flowers bloom in the foreground next to large flat rocks and sunlight forms a dappled pattern on the forest floor. Trees are what you make them. No puny trees have been scratched into these paintings with the base of a watercolor brush! Some artists paint real trees, even if the scene is imagined.

Deciduous trees are delicately beautiful in the spring just before their leaves come out fully, when the dark skeleton formed by the branches is still visible. The leaves are various shades of pink, red, pale green, darker green, yellow ochre, and light yellow. If you make sure tree branches and trunks always become progressively larger as they get closer to the ground, your trees will look right. Skinny trees, like Monet's poplars, might not be a lot larger at the bottom, but they aren't smaller either. Remember to bring some branches around toward the front of the tree. When you think the tree is finished, add a darkened "V" at the crotch of each of the branches to better define where they meet the trunk or another branch. If you become bored painting trees from a distance, sketch one while lying underneath it. People like tree paintings. I once met a painter who only painted pictures of birch trees all day, every day, and claimed to make a living doing it. Talk about a job! Nevertheless, his paintings were very appealing and apparently sold well.

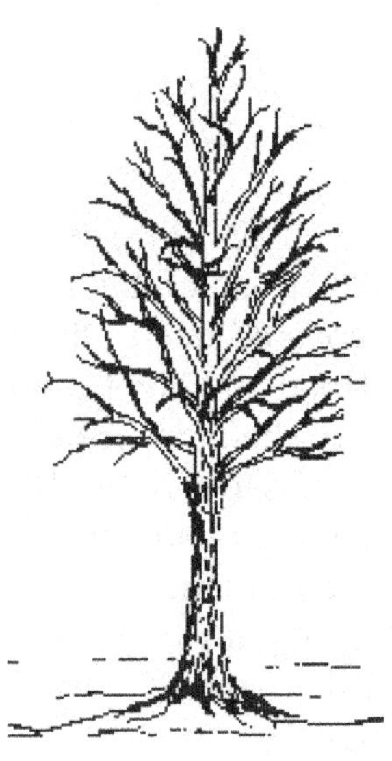

Trunks and branches become larger toward the ground.

Bark is one of several things that helps us differentiate trees. To paint a generic bark in watercolor, brush clear water on the tree branches and trunk. When the shine flashes off, paint them pale Prussian blue. After it dries, paint small, vertical, fatter in the middle, wavy streaks with clear water. Add a drop of brown at the top, and a little Payne's gray at the bottom of each streak. Load a brush with each color. Load another with water. Have a larger, dampened brush ready to soak up the excess. The wavy streaks are the cracks in the tree bark. Adapt this technique for the bark of the specific tree you are painting. After the trunk is filled up with the wavy streaks and has dried, glaze over it with brown or gray followed by green on the lower trunk to indicate moss. Give it volume by shading the left side of the trunk and the branches. Cracks in the bark are usually less prominent on the branches than on the tree trunks. Being able to paint an identifiable tree will enhance your work. It is fun to paint a tree and have someone say "Oh, that looks like a sycamore," when that is what you intended. The bark of the sycamore is different from other trees with its softly dappled yellow ochre, green, pink, and gray tones. Sycamores often grow near springs or creeks. Trees have different shapes and heights. When painting different varieties of trees, it might help to get out the encyclopedia and research them. Then, when you go outside, you will know the trees you are painting and drawing.

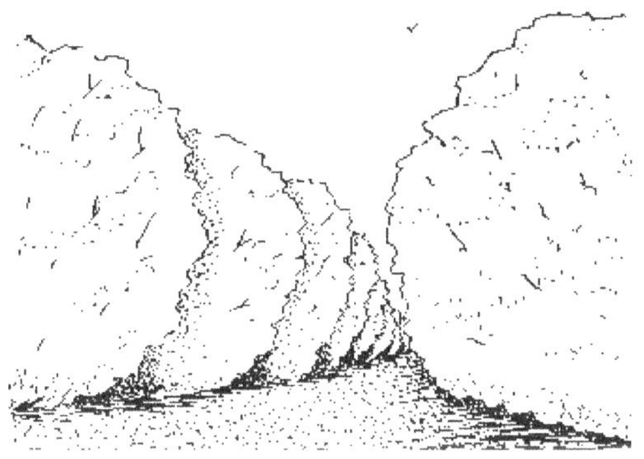

Profiles of Brush along the Road

To paint trees or shrubbery along the roadside, draw their profiles. Decrease their size as they recede in the distance. Put a little shadow between each one. If all the shrubbery is similar, it may seem difficult to see their profiles, but with a little practice you will be able to do it.

It's easy to draw one leaf, but when you want to paint a whole tree, a little voice in your brain will tell you that it is highly unlikely that you will draw every single leaf individually. The job becomes easy if you paint clumps of leaves or needles with pieces of branches showing between them. Let a few tiny branches extend beyond clumps. Make the edges of the clumps irregular, as if some leaves or needles were poking out into the air. If there is a building in back of a tree in the painting, let some of its color show in the gaps between the branches and leaves. Painting clumps works well with blossoming fruit trees and evergreens, too. Evergreens may have skinny horizontal or drooping clumps that let the tree trunk show intermittently. Take care not to space the visible trunk too regularly, like a dotted line, as it goes up. Adding shadow to the lower parts of the clumps of leaves or needles will give them a feeling of weight and form, and the branches should have some from the leaves above.

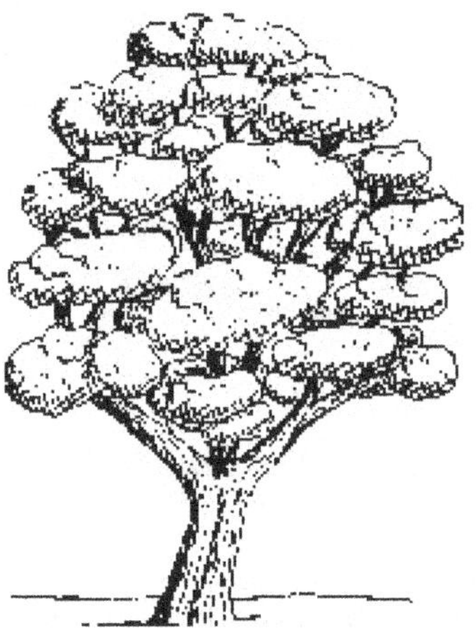

Apple Tree with Exaggerated Clumps of Leaves

Paint leaves in watercolor by brushing clear water on one clump at a time. When the shine flashes off, drop in various colors of your choice and their complements. When it's dry, go back into the light areas and add branches or color from buildings or leaves that are on the far side of the tree. Add darker or more intense colors and shadows to the bottom of the clumps. Paint some closer together and use irregular texture to indicate leaves.

Flowers

Flowers make great painting subjects. Georgia O'Keefe (1887-1978) painted huge ones and critics praised their sensuality. A good painting of flowers is almost as good as having the real thing and it doesn't have to be watered or thrown out. They have hard and soft edges, shadows, highlights, and interesting shapes. Van Gogh's oil paintings of straggly, rough sunflowers are beautiful in spite of themselves. [Ref. 5, p. 24] They are in a substantial pottery vase. Their huge stems would never have looked right painted in a small, dainty container. If he had used a glass vase, the stems would have appeared to move slightly to the left or the right as they went into the water. Van Gogh achieved balance in his painting by letting the flowers touch the top and sides of the painting. The vase is almost at the bottom of the picture. Van Gogh also painted other flowers. His famous picture of irises fills up the canvas with wonderful colors. [Ref 5, pp.56, 57] If you don't have real flowers, a seed catalogue will have close-ups that can be helpful with details. Draw the flowers carefully and paint the details of the blossoms, buds, and stems. Separate them by adding shadows from higher flowers that would fall on each petal, leaf, and stem below. This will create distance between them. Paint a few single petals which have fallen from the arrangement for a more natural look. Whether or not your goal is to be a great flower painter like O'Keefe or van Gogh, it is possible to learn a great deal by painting flowers.

When painting a watercolor of small white flowers or flowers with small amounts of white in them, consider using a masking fluid such as Friskit® to preserve the white space. Keep one brush for use with masking fluid. The masking fluid will eventually ruin the brush no matter what you hear to the contrary. Paint masking fluid on small areas you intend to leave white. Give it a few minutes to dry. Watercolor over and around the masked area. Let the paint dry overnight. Remove the masking by rubbing it off with your fingers. Masking is especially important if you plan to cover the whole floral area with a background color wash before you paint the flowers. Draw the leaves and flowers that will be covered by the color wash with a darker pencil line than you would normally use because the lines will be harder to see after you cover them with the watercolor wash. If the wash is the petal color, add darker green or blue to the background around each flower. Paint large areas of white flowers by painting the negative space around them and adding light colors and shadows to the whites later. Watercolor paint that comes in contact with masking fluid sometimes forms a hard edge when it dries if too much water has been used with the paint. After you remove the masking fluid, soften the hard paint edge by touching it with water and rubbing gently with a damp quarter inch wedge brush. Pat it with a paper towel to lift off color. Rinse the brush with clean water and repeat the process.

Remember that a good drawing, beginning with a thumbnail sketch, is a crucial first step in producing any good artwork. Once the design is solid, you will be well on your way to creating beautiful floral paintings.

Birds

John James Audubon (1785-1851) remains the gold standard in bird paintings. His paintings are a record of this country's bird life in the early 1800's and are precisely accurate in detail. He shot, ate, stuffed and painted the birds he saw in order to document their existence as he traveled in untamed country. His legacy lives on today in the Audubon Society's work to preserve birds. Even so, today's bird painters need not take a back seat to him.

"The "Birds in Art" competition sponsored every year by the Leigh Yawkey Woodson Museum of Wausau, Wisconsin has, at least once, resulted in a book called "Birds in Art, The Masters." It contains paintings done by the winners since the contest began in 1976. The art in it provides a model of contemporary excellence for anyone wanting to paint birds in natural settings. One painting of left facing blue jays in front of a pinkish beige background shows two snow covered branches with two of them sitting on one branch while another one sits above them on the second branch. [Ref. 9, p. 71] Their bright blue and black colors are crisp and elegant. After the initial impression, one notices the artistry of the snow covered branches, including some in the distance that are all delicately lighter than the background color. Today photography allows artists to paint birds without harming them. The paintings in "Birds in Art" are accurate in detail and depict natural settings.

Choose a bird in nature or use a bird book as a reference. Draw a circle for the head. Leave some space and draw an oval for the bird's body. Let the neck connect the circle and the oval. Add the wings, feet, and beak. For watercolor, brush a little clear water on the area you want to paint. Keep adjacent areas dry so the colors won't run into them. If the feathers on the breast of the bird are white, add some yellow ochre, light brown, or gray to the edges where you want a little shadow. Do this in any area to show a rounded shape. Use a larger, splayed, damp brush, to pull color towards the center of the breast area so that it begins to look soft, fluffy, and curved. If you want to show individual bits of feathery down, paint fine lines of color when the area is dry. Go over the lines with a slightly dampened brush to soften the paint edges while they are still wet. Before the paint dries, lift a highlight off the top of the back of the bird and the head, to show where the light hits it. Don't apply water first when painting fine details, such as the bird's tiny eye, because small areas are hard to control. Leave a white spot on the pupil of the eye as a reflection, or paint it on with white acrylic paint after the rest of the eye is finished. When painting the beak, put in a dark line to indicate where it opens and dark dots where the bird breathes in air. Lift excess water and soften the paint edges. Use a wedge brush to create a highlight on the top and bottom of the beak where it curves. If you observe birds in nature you will be able to recognize typical poses. Shore birds, for example, often sit facing into the wind. If you paint a bird using a book as a guide, try to observe the bird in nature as well.

Birds have universal appeal. I painted several versions of a painting I titled "Small Talk." Two fat little birds on the leafy branch of an apple tree faced each other and appeared to be having a conversation. Another version had two raspberry tinged birds on the thorny, snow covered branch of a hawthorn tree full of red berries. Although small, the paintings were very appealing in wide mats and pretty gold frames.

Rocks

Rocks have infinite variety and yet have many similarities. The coast of Maine has terrific rocks. A trip there just to paint them would not be a waste of time. Take the boat from Port Clyde to Monhegan Island. The artists sometimes have open houses the day the boat comes in. The island is a step back in time. When I was there in the late 1990's the old hotel still used oil lamps that were set in cast iron wall brackets. Go for the day or reserve a room ahead of time and stay longer. Non-painters should bring their own books to read. Look for the best rocks along the shoreline.

When painting a rock in watercolor, lightly draw each section in pencil. Brush clear water inside the lines and let adjacent segments dry before painting the ones next to them. Load three brushes, with Prussian blue, Payne's gray, and Indian red. Keep another brush with a little clear water on it, and a larger, slightly damp one ready to mop up water. The colors you use may vary depending on the type of rocks. When the shine has flashed off, touch various parts of the rock with gray, blue and Indian red paint without using too much water. Leave some areas lightly painted especially if you want them to appear sunlit. Glaze a darker gray shadow over part of the rock after the first layer of paint dries. If your watercolor painting contains many individual rocks, such as those in a stone wall, let each freshly painted rock dry before painting adjacent ones. Paint by skipping from one rock to another. If you paint them in sequence, you may be painting with a looser style or brush stroke when you get to the last one, and the beginning part of the wall will look different from the part you painted last. If you skip around, changes in your painting style won't matter.

After painting all the stones, go between each one with a fine line of dark brown mixed with dark gray and paint the shadows between them. When you have painted a line an inch or two long, dip a large round brush in water, squeeze out the excess, splay the bristles, and while the line is still damp, pull one edge of it into the left side of the rock. Keep a hard edge on the left side of the line and let the right side blend into it. This will give the stones additional shape and fullness.

Add weeds or ivy to a stone wall by drawing them on before you begin to paint. In watercolor, paint lighter things first, and darker things last. In oil painting, paint the dark things first and lighter things last. Believe me, that is a shift that takes some getting used to. A friend of mine who paints in oil paints the lights and darks first as she sees them. As she finishes the painting, she darkens some of the darks and lightens some of the highlights because it gives her work more depth.

What happens when a gravel driveway or a rocky beach is part of your watercolor painting but you don't want to paint every tiny little stone? Paint a few of the closer ones and then use gray, brown, purple, blue or black watercolor crayons for the rest. Dot them on paper and touch them with a slightly dampened or one containing gray watercolor paint to give the illusion of gravel.

Beaches

Artists have always been able to find painting subjects on the beach. A single conch shell makes a pretty painting as does the postcard-perfect sand dune, seagull, and sunset. One might take on a larger task and paint the beach full of colorful umbrellas and sunbathers or kids putting sand in buckets. Ladies wearing dresses and carrying parasols made pretty pictures in earlier times. Paintings of people from bygone eras working on the beach intrigue me, perhaps because they are from a simpler time and show a seriousness of purpose. There is something on the beach for every artist.

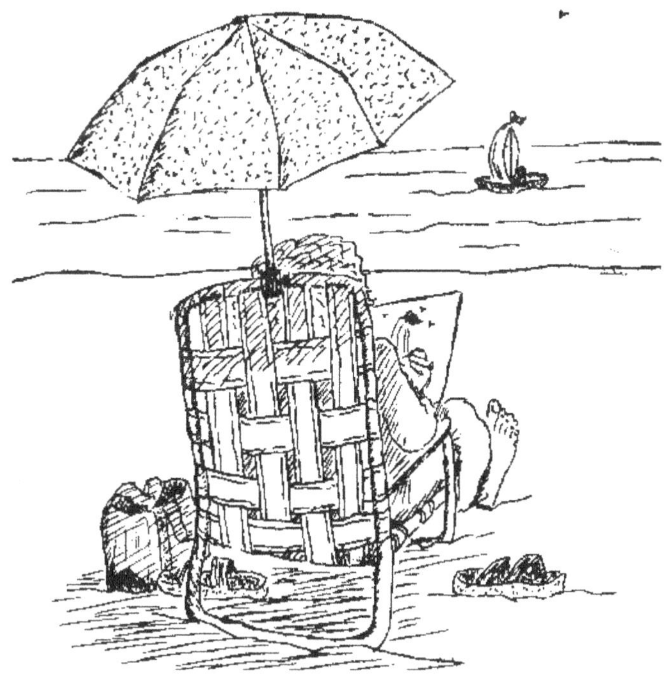

Painting on the Beach

One of my favorite beach paintings of the past is "On the Beach at Scheveningen," by the Dutch painter, Tadama-Groeneveld, (1871-1938). [Ref. 2, p. 34] In this painting two horses and their riders on the left face the sea and are clearly focused on meeting a small ship with billowing sails headed toward them from the upper center. The painting looks as if paint has been applied, allowed to dry, and scraped off repeatedly, a technique sometimes employed by oil painters. Shallow water at the edge of the beach catches bits of reflections of the man and woman on horseback. A close look reveals pink and a streak of cobalt blue amid the ocher, beige, and brown tones of the beach. A heavily clouded sky, with pale blue peeking through it, gives the impression of a cold gray day.

I also like "On the Strand at Katwijk," a small painting by an American, David B. Walkley, (1849-1934) [Ref. 14, p. 120] that shows a man sitting on a horse drawn cart that is stopped on the wheel tracks leading toward us on the left. A woman on foot to the right of the cart is talking to him. A small sailboat is visible in the water in the middle left and a larger ship is being unloaded on the beach at the right. The background is foggy and one can almost feel the chill of the early morning air.

When I paint my own beach scenes, I like to use watercolor crayons (Caran d'Ache Neocolor II Aquarelle) because they give the sand a textured appearance. I draw with them on dry paper and usually go over the drawing with a damp brush. If I have applied the crayon lightly, however, I sometimes paint over the crayon with watercolor paint, without applying clear water first. Either way, keep the surface fairly dry so the colors do not get too mixed together. Too much water mixed with heavily applied watercolor crayon results in mud. Conversely, too much water over lightly applied crayon can make the paint look weak and washed out. Use watercolor crayons anywhere you need texture. They can help portray coal in a railroad gondola car with white flecks of paper showing as reflections on the coal, plaid on a wool dress, small rocks and sand, etc. When you are finished using the crayons on the beach painting, glaze over the beige sand nearest the ocean with pale aqua watercolor to indicate shallow water. You might find beach scenes more meaningful if you paint some activity besides sunbathing. Try painting a beach during the winter or after a storm or some unusual event.

I sketched the beach from a fifth floor hotel room in Ocean City, MD as a hurricane threatened the city. Kids were roller-skating on the boardwalk, using beach towels for sails and letting the 25-35 mph winds propel them along. Birds struggled to fly against the wind. Riptides churned the water and sand. A lone teenage boy with a boogie board stood on the officially closed beach. I sketched as fast as I could because the whole scene was so unusual. When the boy finally summoned the courage to jump in, the current swept him swiftly down the shoreline where he was rescued by life guards. Paint things that interest you. It may surprise you when others appreciate what you have painted.

Atmospheric Perspective

Realistic landscapes need to have depth and atmospheric perspective. Varying the size of objects and the brightness or intensity of colors will give a painting depth. Painting objects and people larger, with more intense colors, in the foreground and smaller, with more faded colors, in the background will produce a sense of perspective. Clouds at the top and flowers in a field in the foreground, should be larger than those found in the center or background of the painting. Flowers in the distance might just be a line of color. The reduction in size is gradual. Same sized objects close to the viewer appear larger than those in the distance. If using a photo as a guide, the brightness or dullness of the colors may not translate well if copied exactly. The photo may have a blue or purple cast that is not present in nature. This is especially noticeable when a painter copies a badly reproduced picture from a calendar. You may need to adjust the colors. The sky near the horizon is usually lighter colored than the sky higher up in the painting. Sometimes an artist will paint a scene, remembered or imaginary, with leafy, dark green hills in the distance when actually, mountains in the distance appear as pale blue, gray or purple. We may know that, close up, the trees are green or gold but we should paint them the pale colors and not let what we know get in the way of what is visible. A little planning and thinking and observing nature will put your landscapes on the right track.

Painting When You Travel

Painters have always traveled. Paul Gauguin (1846-1903) went to Tahiti and produced paintings which were unlike anything being exhibited in France at the time. John Singer Sargent (1856-1925) painted the "blue men" (Bedouins) of Morocco, resplendent in their vivid blue turbans. [Ref. 19, pp. 54-56] American painters traveled to France, Italy, and Germany to study in the early days of this country because there were no well established schools of art here. They painted Venice and other picturesque places. Mary Cassatt (1845-1926) went to France and painted mothers and children in the style of the Impressionists. Childe Hassam (1859-1935) went to Paris and later became America's foremost Impressionist painter. Others traveled to the American West to document it or to show it to magazine readers. Charles M. Russell painted cowboys and Indians. Alfred Bierstadt (1830-1902) painted the great unspoiled scenery. George Catlin (1796-1872) painted Indians in their native dress. Thomas Moran (1837-1926) painted Yellowstone better than anyone. See many of the great Western paintings at the Buffalo Bill Historical Center's Whitney Museum in Cody, Wyoming. Painters don't have to travel, but seeing something new and unfamiliar often provides a fresh view that those who live there and see it every day miss. Many of these painters were people with free time and few financial worries, or artists who had contracts with publishers.

In today's world, photography has allowed artists of ordinary means to travel and bring the pictures home to work on in our spare time. Good transportation has made trips to distant lands fast and easy. Art magazines advertise leisurely painting trips that last a week or two. Non-painting tours can be very fast paced. I haven't managed to paint much those vacations but I do take pictures. I took a close-up of the carpet in the Blue Mosque in Istanbul and it was a delightful souvenir of the visit. The carpet was new and very soft and plush. We were instructed to remove our shoes and walk on it in our socks or bare feet. At the time I felt a little foolish aiming my camera at the floor. A few years ago, some friends showed us pictures of their foreign trip. Every picture was a panorama of some city. They all looked the same to me. There were no interesting details of anything. Those photos would have been useless to a painter. Don't be embarrassed to photograph whatever looks good to you. If you want to paint something in context you will need to take more close-ups than you think you should as well as some wider shots to get the surroundings. An acquaintance of mine painted a series she called "The Fountains of France." Her narrow painting focus caused her to produce better paintings than she would have if she had painted landscapes of the parks containing those same fountains.

Sometimes a scene will almost paint itself. San Gimignano, Italy, a charming Tuscan town known for its towers, built by residents trying to outdo each other, has a long winding, hilly, main street filled with shops and cafes. I went all the way to the top and found an open iron gate in an ancient stone wall. The gateway framed a beautiful view of rooftops, an umbrella pine tree, and a background patchwork of distant fields and mountains. Sunlit dappled vines grew on the wall around the gate. It was a painting trip and I had time to draw it. I finished the picture at home. It's on the cover of this book.

Packing for a painting trip via air can be a challenge. The instructor may send a list telling you what you bring along. A portable watercolor palette box is small, strong, and travels very well. I found a laptop computer case with wheels and a pull up handle for under twenty dollars at a discount

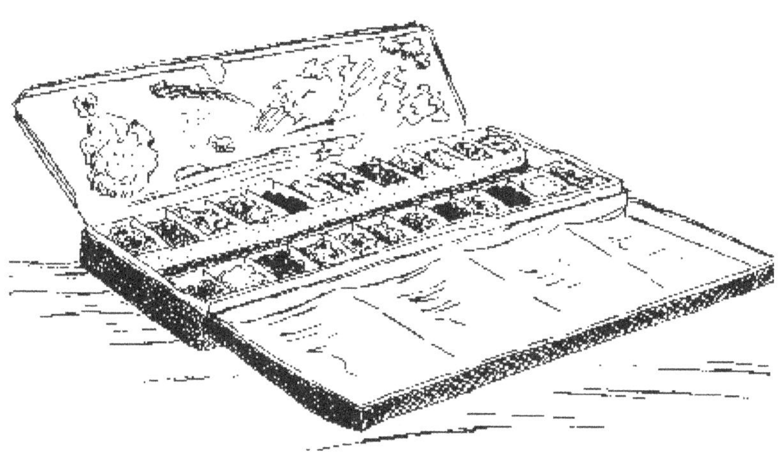

Portable Watercolor Palette Box

store. I packed my art supplies in it. For the trip to Italy I didn't want to risk losing any finished paintings, so I packed only paper that would fit in the carry-on. A small block of watercolor paper and 11" by 15" quarter size sheets fit nicely in the inside pocket. I kept the loose sheets together with a couple of bulldog clips that are also useful for keeping paper from blowing around outdoors. I included my watercolor palette box, plexiglass, grease pencil, ruler, pencils and kneaded eraser. I decided to use regular water, not the distilled water that I prefer at home, and I packed a plastic container for it. Bottled water would have sufficed. I took a wide brimmed hat in a larger suitcase by stuffing it with small items and surrounding it with other clothing. Since we were going to be in cities and planned to paint during the day, I left the insect repellant at home. Be careful not to pack any palette knives, scissors, razor blades, etc. in your carry-on. Keep them in your checked luggage.

Car trips provide more room for art supplies, especially large painting surfaces. I also have more time to paint then because we usually stay in one place for several days. If I sketch on site, using the paper the size I want the finished painting to be, I find that I am more likely to get the size of objects right, and more likely to finish the painting later. Photographs taken on a fast paced trip with a planned itinerary are a great tool, but sometimes they make better reference than primary material. Stonehenge made this clear to me. When I was there, the huge rocks were awesome. If I had had time to sketch them, they would have filled the paper. I didn't. When I got home, and used my photographs, I made a nice painting, but the feeling of being there was not in it. It was a view from a distance. It would have been a different painting had there been time to draw it on larger paper on site. Unfortunately, circumstances often dictate how one will proceed with a painting.

Odds and Ends

- **Matting and Framing**
- **Giclee Prints**
- **Hand Made Paper**
- **Painted Sculptures**
- **Building a Web Site**
- **Art Clubs, Guilds, and Galleries**
- **Bon Voyage**
- **Magazines/Vendors/Bibliography**

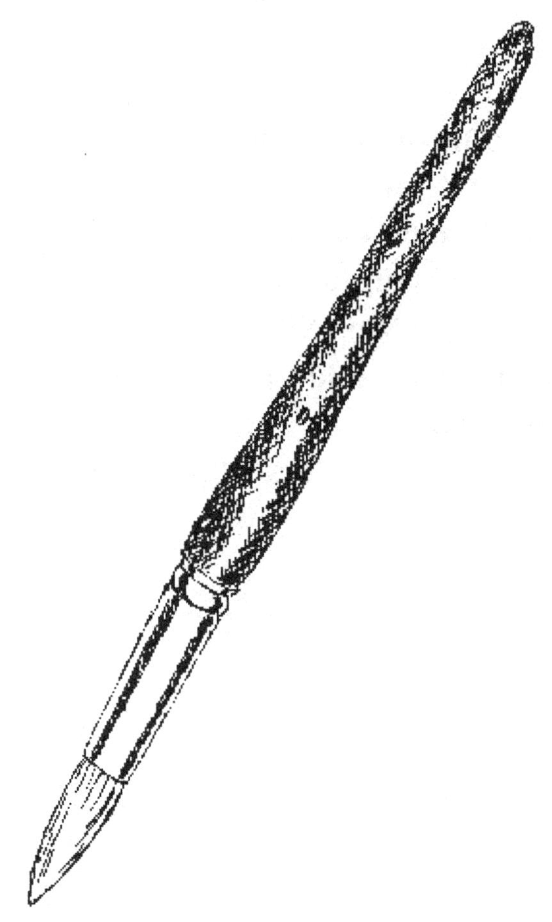

Large Round Brush for Watercolor Painting

Matting and Framing

Commercial frame shops do a great job matting and framing art. Unfortunately professional framing can become expensive if you have many paintings to frame. Reduce the cost by making your own mats, buying frames and glass, and assembling it all yourself. Generally mats are wider on small paintings than on large ones. A two inch wide mat on a small painting will still result in a small painting. Put the same picture in a five inch wide mat, and the work will seem larger and will command its own wall space. Large pictures already have enough size and, therefore, look better with mats that are proportionally smaller. A four or five inch mat on a large painting will work. Mats generally look better in neutral colors and are usually wider than the frame. Mat cutting requires some physical strength. Before you purchase a mat cutter, try those owned by other painters and get recommendations from friends. Mats on vertical subjects should be cut a little wider at the bottom of the frame than on the other three sides to account for the optical illusion called "visual drop." [Ref. 3, p. 24] Make a few practice mats before you try to make one that has to be perfectly done for an important painting. With a little effort you will be able to make nice mats, order wholesale frames, and save money on the cost of matting and framing.

Making double and triple mats takes a little practice. Cut the first (outside, largest, most visible) mat board the correct size to fit the frame. Pencil in the desired mat width on the back on all four sides before cutting the window. Mat width increases with each inside mat. Cut the window in the first mat, with the mat face down, and leave it in place. Cut the outside perimeter of the next mat about half an inch shorter all the way around the outside than the first one.

Apply permanent dry bond adhesive to the back of the first mat. Place the front of the uncut second mat on top of the adhesive and press the mats together. I use Chartpak®'s permanent dry bond adhesive. It comes on a waxed paper strip and is applied with a little wheeled applicator. The non-permanent kind may eventually slip. The adhesive comes off while the paper rolls up on the inside. Cut the second window and repeat the process for the third mat, first cutting the piece of mat board a bit smaller than the other two. They will fit into the frame easier if they are not all the same size. Leave each cut mat window in place until you finish cutting all of them so as to provide support for the next ones.

French mats have thin lines of ink, with paint between them, or strips of patterned paper, available in adhesive strips, on the mat surface for decorative effect. The conundrum is how to get the corners right, especially if the mat is wider on the bottom than on the other three sides. Measure the same distance from the inside of the mat's window on all sides. Pencil in the lines delicately just where they intersect to form the corners. Check the points from each corner with a ruler to be sure they all line up. Use a "T-Square" and an ultra fine permanent marker to draw the lines around the mat window. Position the T-Square so that the transparent part is above the mat so the pen point will not rub against it and smear the ink. Hold the ruler in place and move the pen from one corner point to the next. Paint between the lines with a filbert brush or a round watercolor brush loaded with acrylic or watercolor metallic, karat gold, or other paint. Avoid hard edges by painting with clear water first and adding color while it is wet.

Beautiful fabric covered mats are terrific if you have the time and energy to make them. The most stunning silk mat I ever saw was at the Brandywine Museum in Chadd's Ford, PA. The mat itself was about five-eights of an inch thick and about six or seven inches wide. It looked as though thick foam core board had been professionally cut with a very sharp exacto® knife and covered with cream colored silk fabric. There wasn't a wrinkle to be seen on it anywhere. I thought about trying to duplicate it and got as far as realizing the fabric would have to be placed over the front of the mat, pulled taut and glued to the back. An "X" would be cut across the front of the fabric. The points would then be pulled to the back, over the beveled edges, pulled taut, and glued to the back. I never got around to making it. In the back of my mind I keep thinking I should try it with Velcro®.

When matting watercolors, I find that the top mat will sometimes slip allowing the edges of a painting to show or get caught in the mat. The traditional hinge mat doesn't work for me although it might if I'd cut the window smaller. I place my watercolor painting face up under the mat and carefully turn both over, using masking tape underneath to hold them together just long enough to flip them, then tape the top of the painting to the back of the mat in three or four places with acid free archival tape. The painting now stays behind the mat window without moving around. Due to atmospheric changes in humidity some rippling is normal. The paper should be free to adjust to these changes and should neither be taped down completely on all sides nor should it be glued down to a support. To prevent acidic materials from leaching into the painting, use an acid free backing board or place acid free barrier paper between the work on paper and a non acid free backing board.

Single strength window glass from a local auto glass business is fine for small works under glass. Art organizations usually prefer it. They also like plexiglass or clear acrylic on larger work for exhibition. Non-glare glass is generally not used on exhibited work but you might prefer it in your home if the glass reflects light making it difficult to see the painting. Glass is available that may protect against ultraviolet rays, but always hang artwork out of direct sunlight and never use picture lights. The heat from sun and picture lights can cause cracks to form in oil paintings and can fade watercolors. Use ceiling spotlights as needed when you want to show off your artwork.

Never spray anything directly on the glass covering a painting. Spray a paper towel and wipe the surface, otherwise, the spray can run down to the bottom and seep into and discolor the mat. Use Windex® or a similar product to clean window glass, but do not use it on plexiglass. Instead, use a spray cleaner designed for plastic eye glasses. Using window cleaner on plexiglass will create an ugly film which will destroy its transparency. Never spray anything on an oil painting. Use a feather duster sparingly.

When ordering a frame, measure the exact distance of one short and one long side of the painting, such as 16 x 20." Then check the frame catalogues and order a frame to suit the work. The frame will arrive about an eighth of an inch larger and the painting will fit. Many catalogues will send a free piece of a frame if you want to check color or see how it will look with your painting. Frame catalogues often sell backing boards, clips and other accessories that will make framing your work relatively inexpensive and easy to do.

Giclee Prints

Giclee (pronounced "she-clay") is French for "spurt or squirt" and is an apparent reference to the way the ink squirts onto the paper. A giclee print is a reproduction of art work produced by scanning an original into a computer and printing out the image on fine art paper or canvas. Originally giclee printing was done on an Iris® printer but some other commercial printers now have the same capability. The pigmented inks may keep their brilliancy from fifty to two hundred years or more. Very often a giclee print will look brighter, cleaner, and better than the original painting.

Minimize or completely disguise mistakes or damage on original art such as a coffee stain or a hole by pointing out the damage to the technician who can "copy and paste" good parts of the painting over the offending spot so the giclee print will show no sign of damage. This works especially well if there is a defect in an area such as the sky, or a tree, or any place where cutting and pasting with the computer is easy. The original, of course, stays blemished, but the print, fixed on the computer, will be just fine!

The price of the print is based on its size, not that of the original. If the original is too large to scan, or scan and piece together, you will need to have the work photographed and a transparency made. Once the original or transparency is scanned, specify the size of the print. Note that saying the print should be fifty percent of the original size will mean different things to different people and will illustrate the difference between how artists and engineers think. The giclee technician will measure fifty percent of each side of the painting and produce a print that is twenty-five percent of the area of the original. To get a print half the size of the original, request it about seventy-one percent of the original size. The cost is figured on a per square inch basis of the print.

You may be able to sell your giclee prints. At the very least, you can give them to family members and friends so that they will be able to enjoy your work even if they don't have the original. My grandmother painted over twenty oil paintings that have survived. They were left in a box for thirty-five years after she died. When my mother found them, she gave them to me. I let the grandchildren choose two or three originals apiece. If they wanted more, I gave them giclee prints so everyone could enjoy the paintings they liked.

Artists who sell multiple copies of their work may find giclee prints to be an acceptable alternative to lithographs. While lithographs cost less per piece, a fairly large investment may be required to do a lithographic printing because the printer's minimum can be several hundred copies. Giclees cost more per piece, but the giclee printer's minimum is one copy. Giclees are stored on a computer and can be printed on the same roll of paper as the work of other artists. This also eliminates inventory storage problems. After the work has been scanned and the giclees made, you might ask the giclee print technician for a disk containing Jpegs or Tiffs of your paintings so you can keep track of your work. Purists don't call giclees "prints" at all and consider them reproductions. With their vibrant colors and technical possibilities, giclees are terrific by any name.

Hand Made Paper

Commercially produced papers have a certain uniformity about them and, even if they have an unusually beautiful pattern or color, they still have a predictable flatness and come in standard sizes. You can create beautiful paper in unusual shapes and colors by making it yourself.

It is possible to make paper of any size by using one small framed screen. Don't be confused by stores and catalogues that make you think you will need different sizes of screens just because they are for sale. Buy or make as many as you want, but you really need only one. Build and layer by overlapping sheets of wet paper to get the final size.

Many cotton based things, probably including lint, can be used for making paper. One of the best is abaca paper which is available in art catalogues. Tear it into tiny pieces and then peel them apart as much as you can. Soak the pieces in water for twenty-four hours. You will need a work area where you can get a very watery mess going without ruining the room. Put one cupful at a time in a blender, add more water, and pulverize. This is very hard on a blender. I burned one up doing this. If you get serious about making your own paper, buy a Hollander, an expensive machine that will blend large quantities of abaca paper and turn it into pulp. Pulp is also available already softened and in the right consistency but it can spoil quickly and, when it does, it emits an extremely unpleasant odor. Pour the blended mixture into a bucket or a cooler big enough to allow you to dip the framed screen down underneath the paper pulp. Lift it up and out. It will be covered with the pulp. Another way to do this is to place the screen over a pan and ladle the pulp from other bowls onto it. This is a good way to make multi-colored sheets. Add watercolor paint to the pulp mixture to color it.

Make batches of different colors. Build and overlap them. Use a wide mouthed pastry bag filled with paper pulp to paint bands of color on sheets of wet hand made paper. Press the bands into the paper and squeeze out the water. Flip the paper pulp lined screen out onto a flat, waterproof surface. Press the paper flat with the back of the screen to produce a deckled edge. With the screen on top of the paper, press a slightly dampened sponge on it to remove excess water. Squeeze out the sponge and repeat until there is no more water left in the paper. It is probably a bad idea to pour the excess water down the drain. If you do, at least strain it well first. Better yet, throw it outside.

Emboss hand made paper by pressing the paper against a textured surface as it dries. Prepare the surface by laying string, cheesecloth, leaves, and twigs or whatever you can find, on a piece of cardboard. Paint several coats of matte medium over it. Let it dry thoroughly. The resulting textured surface is called a collograph. Lay the collograph on top of the wet paper. Some artists use a manually operated, hydraulic press to squeeze the water out of the paper pulp while it presses the design into the paper. Attain the desired result by pressing the paper long enough and hard enough so that the texture remains embedded in the paper when it dries. For a less expensive, less labor intensive way to get the water out, flip the pulp filled screen onto felt fabric that has been placed on a Formica® counter top. When the excess water has been absorbed, flip the paper onto the counter, place the collograph on top and press it flat topped by a piece of plexiglass held down by books or other heavy objects. Mop up the remaining water. Let it dry.

I saw a very arty looking paper bowl made of beige, yellow, hot pink and turquoise hand made paper at an art club meeting. It was decorative and beautiful but, of course, would not hold anything heavy or wet. The artist had painted colorful wet paper pulp from a pastry bag on wet sheets of paper. She then placed the wet paper around the inside of a glass bowl, layer by layer, until the inside of the bowl was covered. When it was in place she pressed plastic window screening around the inside of the wet paper lined bowl and pressed a slightly dampened sponge against the screen. Each time the sponge absorbed water from the paper, she squeezed it out and repeated the process. The paper held its shape as it dried. The artist had placed colorful strings in the paper pulp. They came out over the edges of the bowl and the effect was outstanding!

If you plan to write on or paint handmade paper, add laundry sizing to the liquid pulp or spray the finished dry paper on both sides with a workable fixative. (Do it outside and wear a respirator.) If you want to paint on the dried paper with watercolor, while leaving parts of it the original color, make a masking solution by carefully heating up a mixture of half beeswax and half paraffin on very low heat. Stay with this mixture while it warms. Do not let it get too hot. Heat it just until it becomes liquid enough to brush onto the paper. Use a brush you don't care about. After it cools, paint on the paper with watercolor or write on it with permanent marker. Remove the masking by ironing it on low heat with a clean piece of brown craft paper between the masked area and the iron. With every pass of the iron, put clean paper over the masked area until all or most of the wax is lifted and absorbed into the brown paper.

Sometimes, if handmade paper has not been pressed quite flat, it may be better suited for the outside cover of a card rather than the inside. Make an ornate greeting card by sewing or gluing buttons, lace, ribbons, beads or other decorative things to the paper. If the hand made paper is sufficiently sized or spray-fixed with a workable fixative, and pressed very flat, you will be able to write on it. To dress up handmade paper, paint it with gold or silver watercolor paints. Spray it again with a fixative to minimize tarnishing in the case of silver and metals other than genuine gold. There are many ways to decorate hand made paper. Let your imagination guide you!

Painted Sculptures

Hand made sculptures are fun to make. It's a nice change of pace, too, although it is somewhat hard on one's hands. To make interesting small sculptures without chipping away at a marble block, gather together some flat rocks or metal trays or bowls, newspapers, duct tape, wire mesh, florists' wire, picture hanging wire, plaster gauze, water, and acrylic artist's paint. (Medical supply plaster gauze is usually cheaper than art supply plaster gauze.) Imagine the shape of something you would like to create. Assemble the rocks or metal together in that shape. Wrap them in newspaper and tape it all together with duct tape. Refine the shape by wrapping wire mesh over the taped paper. Sew it together with florists' wire. Securely tie in the hanging mechanism. (I like to use picture wire that comes encased in plastic tubing.) Cut the plaster gauze in strips about an inch wide. Soak them in water, a few at a time for a minute or so, just until they become slimy. It gets messy. As the strips get slippery, overlap three or four layers of gauze strips on the wire mesh one layer at a time. Let the whole thing dry completely, until it no longer feels cool when touched with the top side of your fingers. It can take days. If it needs to be smoothed, sand it lightly with fine sandpaper. The surface is attractive either way. Draw on and paint the sculpture, one side at a time, with acrylic artists' paint. Let it dry and hang it up! Decorate hand made sculpture with beads, feathers, or other materials by pushing holes through the dried plaster with an awl and sewing decorations on with florists' wire. I made handmade sculptures of a fish, a bird, a cake, and a crowned head. Someday I may try making a tray or bowl, which could be the best idea of all for this medium.

Building a Web Site

- **Keep it simple.**
- **Plan each page on paper before using the computer.**
- **Take a two night web building class as continuing education at a local community college.**
- **Buy web building software such as MS Front Page (optional but very useful).**
- **Scan and save art or photos to documents file as jpegs.**
- **Keep the font size at least 12 point or larger.**
- **Insert tables and place photos in them; save.**
- **Plan text and background page colors.**
- **Put text in web document with art or photos; save.**
- **Insert hyperlinks to pages and other web sites.**
- **Choose a free or paid web host.**
- **Insert hit counter or other options.**

A web site consists of scanned and saved pictures and text that are uploaded to a web host that makes the site accessible to the world. Keep it simple and easy to navigate. Build the site in its entirety, first on typing paper and then on the computer, before uploading it. Make pictures of artwork very small on paper, about one by two inches, because they will be small on the web page if you use web building software's thumbnail feature. Thumbnails make the site load fast and visitors can click on the small picture to see an enlarged one. This can be done without web building software by sizing the picture very small when you scan it, and inserting a hyperlink to a large version of the same picture on another page.

A "page" of a web site can be made any length, but should be no more than one to three hits of the page down button. The easiest way, but not the only way, is to buy software like MS Front Page. Put the icon on the desktop and click on it. Click on file/new/web. As each page is finished, save it with a name. Insert a table before inserting pictures on a page. Photos not inserted in a table can wander all over the page. They do not stay where you want them. Begin the next page by clicking on file/new/page. Prepare a table of contents page and save it as index.htm or index.html depending on your system's requirements. When all the pages are finished and saved, insert a table on each page with two cells. Type "next page" in one cell and "home page" in the other. Do "previous page" if you like, but the "back" button on your computer should do that without any effort on your part. Make as many links as you think you need. Highlight "next page" and click on insert/hyperlink. A hyperlink tells the computer how to get to a page or another web site. Highlight each listing in the table of contents and insert a hyperlink to the page each refers to so web visitors can get around the web site. Type in the name of the next page exactly as you named it when you saved it. If you can't remember the name, click on "choose file" and find it. Do this on all the pages so the viewer can get back to the table of contents (index) page or to the next page easily.

Many artists now have web sites and some may sell art from them, but it has been my experience that a web site serves mostly as a portfolio. Linking your site to others and letting them link to yours is the best way to get it known. I took a couple two-evening classes at local colleges and built my own web site a few years ago. It took only a couple of weeks. It's web host is addr.com and its address is http://www.rockinggrannyfineart.com. It gave me a terrific feeling of accomplishment to build and publish the web site. It's not free, but it's about the price of having a gourmet coffee once a month. Build a free site, if you prefer, by going to geocities.com, Rootsweb.com, or find one at FreeWebspace.net. These sites allow pop up ads.

Choose background and border colors for tables and cells. If you plan to insert a horizontal bar of color, and it doesn't show up when you upload your web to the web host, go back in and hit the space bar a few times in the color bar as if you were typing text in it. For some reason, this fools it into thinking that there is text or something important in the bar and that the background is useful, and so it shows up!

When the web site is the way you want it on your computer, go on line to your chosen web host and sign up. That site will explain how to upload your web. Note that the user name usually ends up being the name of the web site. Make sure you upload each photo file individually. Even if pictures are on your web on your computer, they may not show up on the on line site unless the photo file is also uploaded or unless you are using web building software such as Front Page that does it for you. The web host will explain how to insert a hit counter. The hit counter is a number that tells you how many times people have clicked on to your web site.

Examine your site by both going on line the regular way to its web address, and by previewing it in browsers provided by your web building software. Sometimes a site will look right in one browser and wrong in another one. Light colored text on a dark background may not show up at all. If things don't look the way you think they should, go over each table, cell, and photo and make sure you saved everything the way you wanted it. You may have to do some trial and error work to see what solves the problems. The whole process can seem very confusing at first, but when you figure it all out, it just snaps together like a Tupperware® lid!

Art Clubs, Guilds and Galleries

Almost every area of the United States has an art club today. If there is no club near you, you might want to start your own. Art clubs function, as do most clubs, with officers, a newsletter, nominal annual dues, and meet somewhere that is free or available for a small donation. The only requirement for joining is an interest in art. A typical meeting begins with a business followed by an artwork "show and tell." Members enjoy non-alcoholic refreshments followed by a program consisting of slides or a painting demo. I remember the first time I went to an art club meeting. I enjoyed hearing people talking about colors, shadows, and paint. I had been reading about art but didn't know any other painters. Art clubs sponsor exhibits of members' work. If you don't know how to get in touch with an art club near you, call a local library, senior center, or newspaper. They may have a contact person available. Otherwise, go to exhibits listed in the paper and talk to artists who will know where the local art clubs meet.

Guilds are more prestigious and may have exhibits in fancier venues. They require prospective members to "jury in" by submitting paintings or slides. They usually require three pieces of similar size, same medium, similarly framed artwork. Most of them do not want to see three very different examples of your work. They have classifications of membership. Some are signature members, meaning they have been "juried in" to their exhibits a certain number of times within a certain number of years, and have earned the right to put the letters, signifying membership in the guild, after their name. They also charge annual dues, and often make already accepted members "jury into" exhibitions. A new artist typically joins an art club. Later, when the artist is better known, he or she might join a guild. Sometimes artists apply many times before being accepted as a guild member.

Shipping artwork to exhibitions can mean building a heavy wooden crate or taping up a cardboard box and hoping the art will make it to the show in one piece. There are better reusable containers available. Air Float Systems makes a cardboard box with a reinforced body and "egg crate" type foam packing, including a cut out area for a framed painting. The boxes are easy to open and close. They come in a variety of sizes. While they seem expensive at first glance, the fact that they can be used more than once and opened easily makes them a reasonable alternative to heavier crates and makeshift boxes. Please refer to the list at the back of this book for more information.

Many artists show their art in galleries. Galleries have different styles and follow different business models. I perceive the most successful ones, from the artist's viewpoint, to be owned by the artist. The artist-owner can showcase his/her own work and the work of others. Some galleries take a percentage of the selling price. Some charge the artist to have a solo show and to print cards as well as the gallery's loss of income if nothing sells. Some go out of business over night. Know the gallery well before you leave work there, and you may want to tie up certain legalities before you consider exhibiting in order to protect yourself should the gallery close with your paintings behind locked doors.

Summer festivals provide artists with another way to sell lithographs, giclees and originals. I've never tried it. It seems like hard work, but it might be exciting and fun with a partner who could help with it. Most festivals require a booth and charge a fee and are generally held outdoors. The booth should provide shade from the sun and protection from rain."

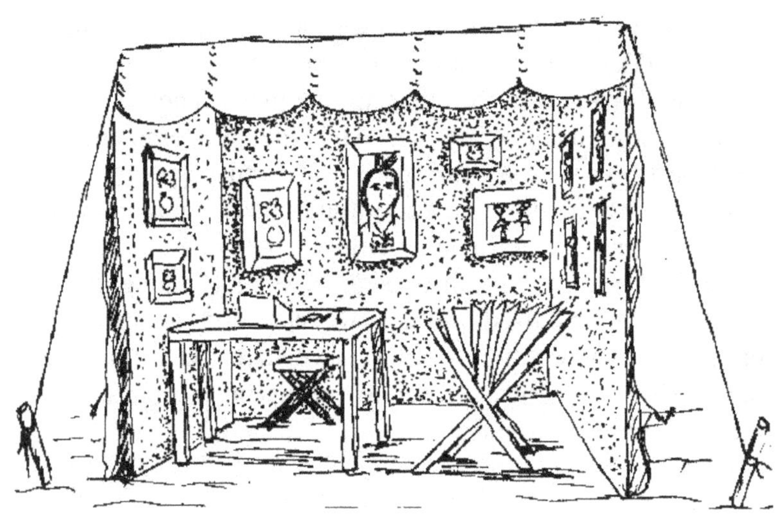

Summer Festival Booth

Be sure to get a tax ID and collect and pay applicable sales taxes if you decide to sell at festivals. Sales should cover your expenses and give you an income as well. Check with specific festivals in your area for their requirements.

Bon Voyage

Just as the Greek poet Kavafis described the journey to Ithaka as one to be enjoyed, I hope your journey through life, painting and doing art related research, will become rich in knowledge and insight as the years pass. Learn to draw well, then paint. The famous quote bears repeating "A good drawing will never be a bad painting and a bad drawing will never be a good painting." Let art take your mind off the daily routine and add a new dimension to your being. Combine it with other personal interests and you will find plenty of painting subjects. Make art about the things that interest you. Paint flowers or barns when you want to and don't be dissuaded by those who say that serious artists don't paint them anymore. Suspect their motives. Perhaps these detractors cannot draw flowers or barns, let alone paint them. Translate scenes of beauty or tragedy into art that moves you and it will move others. You may create many ordinary paintings with great effort and one day paint a great painting easily without realizing its importance. Even if you never paint a masterpiece, relish your painting life. I hope this book will help take you, with art as your companion, on an enjoyable trip that lasts for years! Bon Voyage!

Magazines

Teaching magazines:
American Artist: aart@kable.com or 1-800-745-8922

The Artist's Magazine: www.artistsmagazine.com or
1-800-333-0444

Interesting articles and paintings:
American Art Review: www.amartrev.com or
1-760-738-1178

Art & Antiques: www.ArtandAntiques.net or
1-815-734-1162

Art News: www.artnewsonline.com or 1-800-284-4625

Art in America: www.artinamericamagazine.com or
1-800-925-8059

Vendors

Re-useable shipping boxes:
Air Float Systems, Inc. 1-800-445-2580; fax:
1-800-562-4323;
Air Float Systems, Inc., P. O. Box 229 Tupelo, MS 38802,

Art Supplies:
Cheap Joe's: http://www.cheapjoes.com or
1-800-227-2788;
Cheap Joes's, 374 Industrial Park Drive, Boone, NC 20607
Daniel Smith: http://www.danielsmith.com or
1-800-426-6740;
Daniel Smith, Inc. P.O. Box 82468, Seattle, WA 98124-5568
The Jerry's catalogue: http://www.JerrysArtarama.com,
1-800-U-Artist (1-800-827-8478), in NC 1-919-878-6782;
Jerry's Artarama, P.O. box 58638, Raleigh, NC 27658
Utrecht Art Supplies: http://www.utrecht.com,
1-800-223-9132,
Utrecht Art Supplies, 6 Corp. Dr., Cranbury, NJ 08512
Graphik Dimensions: http://www.pictureframes.com,
1-800-221-0262,
Graphik dimensions Ltd., 2103 Brentwood Street,
High Point, NC 27263

Protective Masks, filters, etc.:
Mine Safety Appliances: http://www.MSAnet.com,
1-800-MSA-2222,
Mine Safety Appliances, P.O. Box 426,
Pittsburgh, PA 15230

Office Supplies:
Staples: www.staples.com or 1-800-3STAPLE

Bibliography

1. **Winston Churchill, His life as a Painter** by his daughter, Mary Soames; William Collins Sons & Co. London, England 1990

2. **Paintings and Sculpture of the Duquesne Club** by David G. Wilkins, Art & Library Committee, Duquesne Club, Pittsburgh, PA 1986

3. **Matting Mounting and Framing Art** by Max Hyder; Watson Guptill Publications, New York, NY 1986

4. **An American Vision Three Generations of Wyeth Art** with essays by James H. Duff, Andrew Wyeth, Thomas Hoving, and Lincoln Kirstein; Published in association with the Brandywine River Museum. A New York Graphic Society Book; Little, Brown and Company, Boston, 1987

5. **The Life and Works of Vincent Van Gogh** by Janice Anderson; Paragon Book Service, Limited; Great Britain, 1994

6. **The Impressionists** by Giles Neret, Wellfleet Press, Secaucus, NJ, 1985

7. **Impressionism and Post Impressionism** Aurora Art Publisher with Hugh Lautner Levin Associates, Inc., Leningrad, 1986

8. **The Henry Holt Retirement Source** by Wilbur Cross, Henry Holt & Co., Inc. New York, 1992

9. **Birds in Art, the Masters** by Brynildson & Hagge, Smithmark Publishers, Inc. New York, 1995

10. **Impressionist Painters** by Jennings, Chancellor Press, London, 1996

11. **Gauguin** Ed. by Rachel Barnes, Brachen Books, London, 1992

12. **Currier & Ives, Printmakers to the American People** by Harry T. Peters, Doubleday, Doran $ Co, Garden City, New York, 1942

13. **Collected Poems** by C.P. Cavafy, Translated by Edmund Keeley and Philip Sherrard, ed. by George Savidis, Princeton University Press, Princeton, NJ, 1975

14. **The Art of the Duquesne Club** by David G. Wilkins, Art & Library Committee, Duquesne Club, Pittsburgh, PA, 2001

15. **Perspective made easy** by Ernest R. Norling, Macmillan Company, New York, 1941

16. **IUP Magazine**, vol. 22, summer 2004, Indiana University of Pennsylvania, 1011 South Drive, Indiana, PA 15701-1087

17. **Rijksmuseum Amsterdam** by Hermine van Guldener, ed. By Berthold Fricke, translated by Yda Ovink, Knorr & Hirth Verlag GmbH, Munich and Ahrbeck/Hanover, 1969

18. **The Watercolors of John Singer Sargent** by Carl Little, Chameleon Books, University of California Press, Berkeley, Los Angeles, London, 1998

Made in the USA
Monee, IL
07 July 2026